UNMAPPED DARKNESS

Finding God's Path Through Suffering

UNMAPPED DARKNESS
Finding God's Path Through Suffering

THOMAS FINCH

MOODY PUBLISHERS
CHICAGO

All Scripture quotations, unless otherwise indicated, are taken from the *Holy Bible, New International Version*®. NIV®. Copyright © 1973, 1978, 1984 by International Bible Society. Used by permission of Zondervan Publishing House. All rights reserved.

Scripture quotations marked NASB are taken from the *New American Standard Bible*®, Copyright © 1960, 1962, 1963, 1968, 1971, 1972, 1973, 1975, 1977, 1995 by The Lockman Foundation. Used by permission.

Scripture quotations marked NLT are taken from the *Holy Bible, New Living Transla-tion*, copyright © 1996. Used by permission of Tyndale House Publishers, Inc., Wheaton, Illinois 60189. All rights reserved.

Scripture quotations marked TEV are taken from *Today's English Version*. Copyright © 1966, 1971, 1976, 1992 by the American Bible Society. Used by permission. All rights reserved.

Scripture quotations marked KJV are taken from the King James Version.

Cover Design: Paetzold Associates
Cover Photo: Getty Images
Editor: Ali Diaz

Library of Congress Cataloging-in-Publication Data

Finch, Tom.
    Unmapped darkness : finding God's path through suffering / by Tom Finch.
    p. cm.
    ISBN-13: 978-0-8024-6750-8
    1. Suffering—Religious aspects—Christianity. I. Title.

BT732.7.F56 2006
248.8'6—dc22

2005036207

We hope you enjoy this book from Moody Publishers. Our goal is to provide high-quality, thought-provoking books and products that connect truth to your real needs and challenges. For more information on other books and products written and pro-duced from a biblical perspective, go to www.moodypublishers.com or write to:

Moody Publishers
820 N. LaSalle Boulevard
Chicago, IL 60610

ISBN: 0-8024-6750-4
ISBN-13: 978-0-8024-6750-8

1 3 5 7 9 10 8 6 4 2

Printed in the United States of America

This book is dedicated to
my wife, Pat,
the woman of faith who inspired it
and who now knows the ultimate reality
of "Christ in you the hope of glory."

It is also dedicated to
my three sons
who have traveled
with me on this journey.

Above all,
may the God of all grace,
the God of all comfort,
be glorified both now and forever.

CONTENTS

"When the foundations are being destroyed, what can the righteous do?"

■ PSALM 11:3 ■

THE STORM:
WHAT IN THE WORLD
IS GOING ON?

THE DAY BEFORE I TOOK the exam for a stock-broker's license, my wife was admitted to the hospital with weakness and dizziness. Pat and I had been married for more than twenty-five years, and her hospitalization weighed heavily on my mind. In spite of her condition, she had my family tell me they were just doing tests and that I needed to stay home and study. The next day I took the four-hour exam and passed, not knowing that a much greater trial was yet to come.

Following the exam, I rushed to the hospital to see my beloved wife. Things did not seem right as I entered the room. A somber aura hung like a cloud over her bed.

After family members greeted me, they took their leave so I could be alone with Pat. I kissed her and took her hand. She could hardly talk.

Then, with speech a bit slurred, she said, "Honey, it's in my brain."

"*What?*" I asked dumbfounded.

"The cancer!"

Tears welled up in my eyes and then flooded across my face. The thought that the one I loved the most would not always be there felt like more than I could bear. Everything was about to change, and I could do nothing to stop it. The reality struck like a razor-sharp arrow piercing into the center of my heart. How could this be? *Why?* Pain shot through every part of my body and spirit. What was happening to my wife? To us? To our sons? To me?

A few minutes later, the doctor came in and took me to one of those sequestered rooms where they share bad news. After we sat down, the doctor said, "Your wife has terminal brain cancer. It's inoperable. She has four to six months to live. I'm sorry. We've begun to give her intense radiation treatments to the brain." Again, I wept.

Pat had previously battled colon cancer, and after an operation, chemotherapy, and radiation, it appeared that she was close to being cured. But now the cancer was back, and not much could be done. My world was shattered. Hope was crushed—the doctor gave no reason for hope.

Just four months after that day in the hospital, my wife was taken from this world.

During the following time of heartache, I reflected on an event that had occurred months before. In order to put bread on the table, I took a new job—a temporary career change. We had prayed for God's will and stepped out in faith to follow where we were led, moving to a new location halfway across the country. In the time of transition, my wife would make my lunch, and occasionally she included a note. The last note she wrote said, "I love you, honey! God is in control of everything." We believed that and lived that. One time when we were talking on the phone, she said, "You must write about the reality of a sovereign God in a fallen world." I did not know I would experience the depths of that fallenness so soon. We were about to have a serious encounter with pain, sorrow, and death itself.

As if caught in the eye of a hurricane and not knowing where I would be dropped, my life and its foundations were being shaken to the core. Those were the stirrings, the swirling storm winds, which would blow at ferocious speeds against the house of my life. This storm was like no other I'd ever experienced. The storm itself would end, but the devastation left in its wake would remain.

Before we go any further, I want you to know why I am writing this book. It is inspired by what happened to my wife and me, but it is much more than that. I have sought to please and serve God with every ounce of my strength. I am not unfamiliar with grief, having experienced it even before my wife's death. I was a senior pastor for years and was well acquainted with the suffering people experience as well as with the suffering portrayed in the Hebrew and Christian Scriptures. When Pat's terminal illness hit us, I knew what was happening to us was not totally unique and that all people encounter the harsh realities of life through painful experiences. I was launched on a journey in search of what is "really real"—the ultimate realities. In the process one discovers what remains true about God and life regardless of our experiences —good or bad, pleasant or painful. This book is about traveling into the heart of God amidst great pain. It is not meant to be read quickly or lightly, but the thoughts offered are for readers to reflect on.

UNDERSTANDING THE
ULTIMATE ORIGIN OF SUFFERING

I, like many others, have said, "Things should not be this way. It's not right, and it ought to be different. How did I get into this pain?" Suffering involves an innate understanding of right and wrong and of how things *ought* to be. With that sense come expectations and a quest for a world without suffering—a different world, paradise. We have a desire for what we think would be "the good life," based on what we instinctively believe life should hold.

Interestingly, that is exactly where the Bible starts, describing the origins of a perfect world. In the early chapters of Genesis, there is a marvelous picture of paradise. The living God created the world, and when it was all done He said, "It is good, very good" (see Genesis 1:31). It seems that this idea of paradise—that it is "good, very good"—is universally latent in the minds of all people. Yet we can hardly understand a true paradise because we've never experienced it. But in Eden, there was no suffering, all needs were met, and there was great joy in the presence of God.

Something horrific happened, and the prevailing order drastically changed. The ultimate, deepest cause of suffering is described in Genesis 3. An event took place and mankind, as well as all of creation, would never be the same again. In a sense, this is the story of every one of us.[1] Historically, theologians call this "the fall," and the result was a "fallen world." After this tragedy, the world was plunged into suffering and corruption of all types. Man fell from paradise to pollution and pain; from innocence to guilt and a sinful condition; and from perfect health to sickness, suffering, and death. Suffering would leave a permanent mark on all things.

Let us recount the story. When God created the world,

He put protective boundaries on His creation. His purpose was to provide His creation with safety and order and well-being. He "made the sand a boundary for the sea, an everlasting barrier it cannot cross" (Jeremiah 5:22); and to the sand itself He said, "This far you may come and no farther; here is where your proud waves halt" (Job 38:11).

Likewise, when God created the garden paradise and placed the first man and woman in it, He gave them marvelous provisions, including instructions for life and living with Him. He set the protective boundaries for their safety and order and well-being as He had for all of His creation. It is in the words of God that we find the first hint of suffering, of what would come if this protection were violated. Adam and Eve were permitted to eat from any tree, "but you must not eat from the tree of the knowledge of good and evil, for when you eat of it you will surely die" (Genesis 2:16–17).

At this very early point, the matter of physical suffering is directly related to spiritual matters. A decision prompted by a certain attitude (and act) would bring about a living death. In other words, disobedience can lead to suffering. Before the fall, Adam and Eve had no knowledge of evil because they were in a state of innocence of such matters, and the guiding words of God were for their protection. Evil was like nothing they had yet experienced in their world. As Milton wrote in *Paradise Lost:*

> Of man's first disobedience, and the fruit,
> Of that forbidden tree, whose mortal taste
> Brought death into the world, and all our woe.
> —Milton, *Paradise Lost*, Book 1, lines 1–3

It is important to note the existence of a personal power of evil. Another force was present in the fall—Satan, the tempter, the fallen angel, came and expressed his deliberate anti-God attitude. Adam and Eve were not forced to listen to his counsel of rebellion against God. But they finally listened, and they disobeyed and ate the forbidden fruit, and the rest is the sad saga of fallen man's history.

Loss of the Good

The most basic relationship of all, the relationship with God, was broken due to the fall. "Your iniquities have separated you from your God; your sins have hidden his face from you" (Isaiah 59:2). After Adam and Eve had sinned, God kept His word, and the results of the broken relationship with Him were described. God told Eve she would experience greatly increased pain in childbirth. He told Adam he would sweat through painful toil to provide for his family. And "just as sin entered the world through one man, and death through sin, and in this way death came to all men because all sinned" (Romans 5:12; also see verses 17–19), therefore the sentence of death that was pronounced upon Adam and Eve has been realized ever since by all people everywhere. As the poet John Donne said, "No man is an island, entire of itself. Each is a piece of a continent, a part of the main. . . . Each man's death diminishes me, for I am involved in mankind. Therefore never send to know from whom the bell tolls; it tolls for thee."[2]

Whether or not we acknowledge it, the fact is that since suffering is part of the human condition, we are all fellow sufferers and suffer together. This all-encompassing suffering that we each experience in some way is simply loss of the good, and the eventual loss of life, since death entered the world after the fall. Though our society and culture seem to be fixated on physical suffering, spiritual or internal suffering has been a dominant issue from the beginning of time. In fact, it seems that suffering on the spiritual level is the most painful and devastating because it affects our view of physical suffering as well.

Having identified *sin* as the original and ultimate cause of suffering and the judgment of God, we must look at a common but incorrect conclusion. It is simplistic to conclude that an individual's sufferings are caused by their particular sins. This misconception implies that all suffering is the direct effect of personal, specific sin. This misuse of biblical truth has caused serious damage to many and has given fuel to skeptics. In this paradigm, suffering is viewed in a legal context: where there is specific punishment, there had to have been specific crime.

Because a painful level of guilt readily surfaces in us, we can be inclined to view suffering as the proper application of a legal punishment from God. My precious wife, as she was suffering with cancer, asked me one day, "What did I do? I must have sinned badly."

Pain and hurt are not always the direct result of sin. The biblical account of the humiliating suffering of the patriarch Job is proof that not all pain has its root in the sin of an individual. Likewise, when the disciples of Jesus encountered a man who had been born blind, they asked, "Who sinned, this man or his parents?" and Jesus bluntly answered, "Neither!" (John 9:2–3). While sometimes sin is the cause of our suffering, it is wrong to judge all suffering as the consequence of the sufferer's sin—as Job's friends did. The reason we tend to do this is that original sin and guilt are so deeply and fearfully engraved on our hearts. The awareness that humankind is in a fallen state and is under the judgment of God is real and pervades most religious belief systems.

Regardless of a person's worldview, virtually everyone will agree that we are surrounded by sin, suffering, and disappointment. This acknowledgment is in stark contrast to most people's initial experiences in life. In a child's world, he or she is coddled and cared for, and perhaps even spoiled. Demands for attention are usually met immediately, which only reinforces a child's belief that the world revolves around his or her desires.

But the real world is not as benign. This fact usually arrives as an unwelcome guest fairly early in life. For me, an experience in my youth sticks out as the first particularly painful awareness that life was not going to go as I wanted. I had a dog, Cindi, who was very special to me. One day she ran out into the street and was hit by a car. I remember crying profusely as I carried her back to the house. There was a deep loss, etched forever in my mind.

Every person has memories even from childhood that indelibly leave an impression on him throughout life.

There were other things I saw as a child that did not seem right to me. My grandfather was very active in the work of the Shriners caring for crippled children. Occasionally he would show my father pictures of some of the crippled or deformed children they tried to help with artificial limbs and other medical developments. Though they hadn't wanted to expose me to the reality of what those photographs portrayed, I peeked and saw them. And though I didn't completely understand what I was seeing, I've never forgotten the pain and suffering reflected on the faces of those children.

Like many young people, I had believed that if you were a good person who sought to do what was right, you would not go through tough times. For much of our lives we live in a kind of make-believe world—the child's world of our early days. Step-by-step we are introduced in unique ways to the real, fallen world. Sometimes the introduction comes like raindrops interrupting our plans for a day in the sun. At other times, reality strikes like a deluge, tornado, or hurricane.

The storm will come—hardship of some sort will come to all of us. As one fellow sufferer described it, "Man is born to trouble as surely as sparks fly upward" (Job 5:7).

Just because you build a good life doesn't mean that the winds, rainy days, and storms of life will not come against you. Jesus told the parable (Matthew 7:24–27) of the two men who built houses. The wise one built his on a strong foundation of rock, but the foolish one built his on the sand. When the storms came, the house built on sand washed away, but the one built on the rock stood firm.

It is in a storm, Jesus explained, that the foundation of one's life will be exposed.

REACTIONS AND QUESTIONS

When tragedy strikes, people experience a variety of emotions. In the newness of deep suffering, tears can come quickly and irresistibly. But following the initial outpouring of emotion, a feeling of numbness is natural. This stage of confusing shock can last varying lengths of time. Heartfelt communication with friends or family or God may come to a standstill because of what has taken place.

The next natural response is that of seeking to defend oneself from the reality of this peril. With stoic resolution, some will resolve themselves to being unmoved by the whole situation and put up a wall of silence. This form of denial is natural to some, but ongoing denial and continuing inability to face the situation can have serious consequences in the future.

Other people become angry or filled with despair. Because the heart is emotionally raw and vulnerable, one may lash out at others for no apparent reason. There is a feeling that someone must answer for the state of affairs. The blame can be cast on oneself or others, but at this point, questions begin to be asked.

Four types of inquiries tend to surface. First there are questions about reality itself.

> *"How can these things be?"*
> *"What's going on here?"*
> *"What is reality?"*
> *"What is there to hold on to?"*
> *"Is there any purpose in life?"*
> *"Is there any reason for all of this?"*

Second, there are questions related to oneself. These may sound like:

> *"What did I do to deserve this?"*
> *"I've tried to do good, but why is this happening to me?"*
> *"Did I sin?"*
> *"Why do the righteous suffer?"*

Then there are the God questions.

> *"How can a good God allow this to happen?"*
> *"Where is God?"*
> *"Does He even exist?"*
> *"Is He in control?"*
> *"What is He like?"*
> *"Can God help me?"*

The fourth type of question has to do with the future.

"Why go on?"
"What do I do now?"
"Where am I headed?"
"How do I move on?"

Entering a time of suffering is entering unmapped darkness. The purpose of our journey is to discover the answer to the questions *What does one do when his foundations are shaken or even destroyed?* and *How can we find our way through this unmapped darkness?*

Francis Schaeffer, a great Christian thinker, described it this way. He said that everyone has built a roof over his head to protect him from the blows of the real world—both internal and external. These roofs are no match for the avalanches of rock and stone, which come smashing down upon us in life. The blows of life rip the roof off and each must stand naked and wounded before the "truth of what is."[3] Through testing one begins to realize what his threshold of security is built upon. This is frightening, but as shall be seen, it is also freeing.

One who suffered more than any other said, "You will know the truth and the truth will set you free" (John 8:32). My faith has been tested again and again as I have wrestled with the hard questions. Sometimes there have been fellow travelers with whom I could discuss my questions, but it is difficult for one who hasn't walked this path to effectively communicate with one who is on the journey. To the sufferer, many times it seems as though no one remembers their own times of suffering or understands yours. I invite you to travel with me into the next chapter as we look at some characteristics of the darkness we are up against. By understanding the nature of the problems we face, we can better see what is needed to push through them.

QUESTIONS
FOR REFLECTION

1. How did God describe His creation? What protective boundaries did He set on His creation?

2. What does the author say is the "loss of the good"?

3. Read Matthew 7:24–27. How does the author interpret Jesus' parable? What did Jesus mean? Is this story effective?

4. The author said he was feeling as though he had been "caught in the eye of a hurricane and not knowing where I would be dropped." Have you ever experienced this kind of suffering? With what typical reactions on pages 18–19 can you identify?

"There is a time for every-thing, and a season for every activity under heaven."

■ ECCLESIASTES 3:1 ■

2

DISTURBANCES: REALITY AS WE KNOW IT

Different Times, Similar Questions

DURING THE VIETNAM WAR years, there was a philosophy on college campuses expressed in the words, "Eat, drink, and be merry—for tomorrow we might be shipped out to Nam and die."

Centuries before these students grappled with the perplexities of life, King Solomon, one of the wisest men who ever lived, also wrestled with the meaning of life. He said, "I set my mind to seek and explore by wisdom concerning all that has been done under heaven" (Ecclesiastes 1:13 NASB). What a comprehensive goal! We live in a vast cosmos, and it would be easy to feel like we are just specks of life on a small planet orbiting around a regular star in a typical galaxy. We can view the immense universe and ask, "What is man that you are mindful of him?" (Psalm 8:4).

We wonder if God sees us. Does He care about our

problems? Are our problems worth His attention? The Scriptures answer Yes! Psalm 8 goes on to tell us that God made mankind "a little lower than the heavenly beings and crowned him with glory and honor. [He] made him ruler over the works of [his] hands" (verses 5–6).

No person can say to another, "Hey, you're not really suffering" or "You've got it made, compared to so-and-so." Minimizing or trying to explain away the painful experiences of others is contrary to any kind of genuine caring or compassion and "violates the integrity of that suffering."[4] Though we like to make comparisons, it makes no sense to measure crises in relation to each other, determining that one's problems aren't as serious as someone else's, or even to wonder whether people of ancient civilizations had more painful trials than those of our times or country. What we need to do before we formulate our responses to our individual dilemmas is understand that suffering is universal—all crises are serious, and all affect individuals uniquely.

There are various types of crises that can rock the foundations of our lives. We'll put some of these into seven categories.

1. Crises of Direction

As we move through life, we continue on an uncharted path, a sometimes ominous unknown that can move us to fear. Questions surface such as: *What shall I do? Which way shall I go?*

It is common to seek direction and guidance at times of crossroads of life. Young adults are faced with questions. *What college shall I go to? What shall I study? What job or career shall I pursue?* A person who feels he or she is at the end of the road with a job is faced with the issue of whether or not to make a career change. *When is it wise to take a risk? What about financial security?*

Edith Schaeffer described such a pursuit when she and her husband faced a blinding snowstorm in Switzerland. They had been informed by the authorities that they would have to leave the canton where they were living because of their missionary activities. They started off in the blizzard in their ski clothes, house hunting with little hope left. She remembers weeping and saying, "Now I have to find a chalet within an hour, or we'll be put out of Switzerland." As they made their way through another small town, she heard her name being called. It was a real estate dealer with whom they'd talked days before. He had found a chalet that was for sale. Edith's words are poignant at this point: "Chance? Coincidence? Luck? To us it was a tremendous instance of answered prayer, a wonderful demonstration of the existence of a personal God who deals with His children as individual, meaningful personalities, and in an individual way."[5] At times my wife would remind me of this story, saying, "Remember the blizzard." This story is still a comfort when I don't know which way to go.

2. Personal Life Crises

There are occasions in life when one is faced with what seems like an insurmountable task. Moses felt this way when God called him to lead the people of Israel out of slavery in Egypt. His answer to God was: "Who am I that I should go and do this? Lord, you know I've never been eloquent" (see Exodus 3:11; 4:10). Who hasn't been faced with a difficult situation and in distress said, "I can't do this!"?

It is often even more painful when one is confronted with a situation in which he feels failure or guilt. We live in a society focused on success. Though we seek to remove the feeling of failure by implying that "all are winners" and "no one is cut from the team," the reality is that sometimes there is only one opening and numerous applicants. When faced with rejection, there is a crisis within, a feeling of loss, and a degree of personal suffering.

There once was a powerful man in a prominent position who lusted after a beautiful woman. He spent time with her and eventually had sexual relations with her while her husband was out of town. She became pregnant. Because of his position, and because he was a man of substantial resources, he was able to arrange for the death of her husband and the cover-up. That man was David, the king of Israel (2 Samuel 11–12). When he was confronted with the truth of what he had done, David recoiled in shame. That feeling of real guilt deeply pierced his heart. See his poignant lament in Psalm 51.

Some personal crises such as addictions seem impossible to break. I knew of an alcoholic once who had progressed so far that he would even drink aftershave just for the alcohol in it. He felt there was no escape from the awful reality in which he was imprisoned. He was enslaved by the addiction that eventually cost him his life.

Others have faced horrendous personal suffering be-cause they have been victims of rape, various forms of abuse, the dehumanizing crime of racism, or any number of types of assaults. Self-worth can be seriously harmed or even de-stroyed by these things, and life can seem to be colored with melancholy hues at best, if not dark dismal tones.

3. CRISES OF PERSONAL RELATIONSHIPS

Relational pain is different from physical pain. A frac-tured arm can heal, but a shattered relationship has a great impact on us for a long time.

I remember early one morning when I received a call from a woman in our congregation. Through tears she said, "My husband has been having an affair. He's going to leave me. What do I do? Please come over and talk to him. He's coming to get his things in about an hour."

When I met up with her husband, he, too, was quite distraught. The amazing thing is that out of this awful situation came reconciliation and healing. This took a long time, however. A broken heart, shattered by betrayal, feels some of the deepest suffering and is not so easily healed.

Our society knows well the bitter pain of a broken marriage and the troubled lives that often result. Many children have gone through the loss of one or both parents, or they have faced abuse, absentee parents, or other deprivations. Even if a young person's family is somewhat stable, relational pain is soon to be experienced through interactions with siblings, friends, or members of the opposite sex. When there is a break in one of these relationships, there is an early brush with rejection that is not forgotten.

Whether it occurs among the old, young, or middle-aged, the suffering of loneliness and depression is painful.

4. CRISES OF CONFLICT

Tension and strife are a way of life whenever two or more people interact. It is inevitable that conflict develops in every type of relationship. In the workplace there will be disagreements between staff and management and among fellow staff themselves. As emotions become involved, the feelings become tense and antagonisms develop that can lead to bitterness. Whether it be among religious people in their gatherings, in neighborhoods, the workplace, or families, the wounds received in this type of combat are deep and real.

Slander campaigns and hidden agendas may develop to defeat a presumed adversary. Where matters of principle are involved, antagonists will often go after personal reputation in order to silence that individual. Being the victim of character assassination or vicious rumors and gossip can bring one to the brink of identity crisis and despair.

5. CRISES IN FINANCES

It is well documented that one of the major causes of conflict in marriage is the matter of finances. Numerous couples have sat across from me seeking counsel as financial stress endangered their personal and marital lives. There is nothing like a lack of money to bring a reality check (no pun intended!). Though I did not live through the Great Depression, my parents and their generation have often spoken of the times when there wasn't much of anything to come and go on. Suffering of all types can be caused by a lack of financial stability and resources necessary for daily living. In a culture that is focused on material things and all the entertainment that money can buy, a lack of money can bring even more stress when added to the everyday concerns of making the paycheck stretch. Sadly enough, many believe our worth is gauged by how much money we have.

Financial stress has its opposite side when it comes in the form of great success. Many people who rise quickly to wealth, whether through stardom, prowess as a professional athlete, or by winning a lottery and becoming a millionaire, face a reality they were not prepared to meet. They often crash due to having so much money at their disposal, loss of former friends and the gain of new "friends," and little wisdom concerning how to use wealth wisely. So whether it be with scarcity or abundance, finances can create a confrontation with what a person is basing his life and worth upon.

6. COLLECTIVE CRISES

Each of us is part of a bigger whole—a family, an ethnic group, a religious group, perhaps a company, a community, a nation. Various ethnic groups and nationalities have faced prejudice and discrimination, even terrorism. When these types of crises are experienced, reality strikes with a bludgeon. The awful atrocities of the Holocaust committed by Hitler and his military against the Jewish people and against others are well documented, but discrimination and violence are not limited to that time. Many peoples have and continue to experience these tragedies.

Man-made disasters such as wars or natural disasters such as the ravages of earthquakes and tropical storms all drive whole communities to face the reality of a very fallen world.

7. CRISES OF A PHYSICAL NATURE

All people will face the ultimate reality of physical crises and death itself. Some of the previously mentioned crises may be avoided to varying degrees, but this one is inescapable. When we are young and full of energy, we have little understanding of physical deterioration. This can last until sickness or death touches close to home.

As a younger couple, my wife and I were excited about our dream of having a big, happy family. Our first son was born, and what a joy! But when our second son came into this world, there were problems. I'll never forget the day when we went to the hospital expecting to have our second "bundle of blessing." As my wife was in labor, the doctor asked to see me outside the delivery room. She said there were complications and they were going to have to operate immediately.

Then other doctors rushed into the delivery room. Eventually the pediatrician came out and shared the fact they had almost lost our new son and that he had a serious chromosome problem. Our son never left the neonatal unit at the hospital and lived only one month.

We didn't know all the reasons for this working of God, but we knew the Lord. That made the difference! One thing that happened a short while later helped us to have a little understanding. Shortly after that loss, I became the senior pastor of a church. The church was right beside a hospital. One day the hospital called and asked if I could come over. A couple had just lost their newborn son and needed some help. I could relate to them and minister to them. I could simply say with depth of feeling, *"I understand."*

FACING THE TRUTH

It is only natural for people to respond to crisis and to try to find meaning behind it. But insufficient responses to suffering and evil have always existed. Some people are intrigued by the violence showcased by the movie and television industries. They find entertaining value in such things, perhaps reducing real problems to the world of the imagination. Others believe there are personal forces behind suffering and evil, and try to tap into the invisible spirit world through games, psychics, or mediums. They might think they can find answers to their questions or reverse or influence events. Such activities are not harmless but can dangerously engage evil spiritual forces into one's life.

A greater majority of people simply live in denial of the fallenness of the world. For the sake of a positive attitude, you hear, "Things are great!" or "Everything's fine." Would-be counselors and even some religious people often sugarcoat reality with the words, "It's not all that bad." Rather than help, they actually harm the person who is in pain by not acknowledging the pain of their situation.

Plain and simple, we despise suffering. Simone Weil pointed out a truth, which at first seems shocking, "Our senses attach [to affliction] all the scorn, all the revulsion, all the hatred that our reason attaches to crime. . . . Everybody despises the afflicted to some extent, although practically no one is conscious of it."[6]

I know this tendency to look away from affliction is true in my own life. We would simply rather not see the burdens people carry with them. When I was a pastor and would visit people in the hospital, I loved being in the maternity ward. That was fun! Parents were so happy and excited about the precious new life that had been given to them. But every pastor knows that all hospital visits are not for such joyful purposes. I especially dreaded the oncology ward because of the pain and imminent death. Little did I know then that I would one day be seeing my own wife in that very section of the hospital.

Our technological and generally more impersonal society exacerbates the desire to suppress the reality of suffering. People just aren't spending as much time together face-to-face. If the news shows people in dire circumstances, we can turn the channel. We can skip over articles in the newspaper or in magazines that make us uncomfortable. If a neighbor or co-worker is depressing to us, we can go the other way. But this attitude toward suffering makes the person on the journey feel even more lost and lonely and isolated. We have developed a hesitancy to share deep inner pain because we believe people don't want to hear that there are problems. How often have we answered the question How are you? with a cheerful "Fine!" even if in our hearts we know that isn't true? As the proverb says, "Even in laughter the heart may ache, and joy may end in grief" (Proverbs 14:13).

THE WHOLE PICTURE

Whether one is a professed Christian or not, there is a grave danger: This is the denial of the mortality and depravity of mankind. In the words of M. Scott Peck, we become "people of the lie."[7] Anyone who has read the literature of humanistic philosophy is familiar with the belief that we all are born wholly innocent and good. The denial becomes an attempt to erase the knowledge of the truth of our fallenness from our consciousness as Paul discusses in Romans 1:19–32. This is an escapism, which seeks to mask the pain and throws a cloak of denial over the entire human condition.

We need to look at objective reality and make sense of it. Our culture's postmodern philosophy has often abandoned the quest for truth and "looking at things as they actually are" and instead engages in a sort of make-believe, embracing whatever we think will make us happy.[8]

It is important to start with the reality that we observe and experience. As one identifies the realities in his experience, he can move on to understanding and ultimately knowing the truth about this fallen world. For example, when I accidentally hit my finger with a hammer, it hurts and you will hear a loud, "Ouch!" There are two simple realities to be observed there: (1) I'm alive, and (2) there is pain.

Yes, the reality of being alive is often taken for granted until we encounter a danger that threatens us in some way.

Good and bad, mortal and eternal, make up what is ultimate reality. If we are looking for understanding about our existence, we need to view the *whole* of life. A merely biological or chemical focus on atoms, neutrons, and protons or genes and chromosomes can miss the essence of what it means to be alive. The dismissal of what separates a human being from other living things underlies many of the bioethical issues being debated in our society.

The heart of life is found in the inner, nonmaterial being of man. This may be called one's spirit, person, or soul. In the first book of the Bible we read that God breathed into man's "nostrils the breath of life, and the man became a living being" (Genesis 2:7). The Hebrew word for "living being" is *nephesh* and implies vitality—spiritual power, personality, energy.[9] The uniqueness of man involves desire, intellect, and emotion. Joy is designed to be part of the picture. As Solomon said, "[God] has also set eternity in the hearts of men . . . eat your food with gladness, and drink your wine with a joyful heart . . . enjoy life" (Ecclesiastes 3:11; 9:7, 9; also see Ecclesiastes 3:22 and 5:19). What brings joy to the heart of man—*nephesh*—is marked by a desire different from all others, the thirst for God. "My soul thirsts for God, for the living God. When can I go and meet with God?" (Psalm 42:2). Woven into the fabric of the spiritual part of man is the desire for purpose in life, as well as "paradise" and the "good." These things aren't found without their (and our) source and Creator.

However, as we have seen, something has gone radically wrong. Our ideas of paradise do not reflect our experience of the realities of life in this world. Something has been lost, for suffering is at its core a matter of a "loss of the good." Worse yet, human beings often are responsible for the wrong. As Solomon observed, "The hearts of men, moreover, are full of evil and there is madness in their hearts while they live, and afterward they join the dead" (Ecclesiastes 9:3). If Solomon is right, then we need something—Someone— higher than ourselves to show us what remains concrete when reality turns out different than anything we've ever imagined.

Most people's views of reality, like that of Solomon in Ecclesiastes, have been linked to their doctrine of God. Some people have heard so much "God-talk" that their hearts are hardened and they can no longer hear. Others have decided to avoid serious consideration of the claims of the truths in Scripture because they don't want to be told how to live. And there are those who either have never heard or who have not seriously considered what the Bible says. "Practical atheists" live as if there were no God (see Psalm 14:1).

The horrors and hurt of human suffering can lead to another intellectual but irrational fallacy. Many professed atheists refuse to believe in God because the world is so bad. This view usually comes by progression: First, God is blamed for the condition of the world, since He created life. Then, because it is undesirable to believe in a God who doesn't immediately use His power to remove evil, it is presumed that He does not even exist.

Many of those who are undecided and agnostic about faith have allowed the experiences of evil to become the primary influence shaping their views of reality and God. All, then, is viewed through the darkness and shadows. This becomes a veil that tends to prevent us from seeing Him with clarity. C. S. Lewis warned of this, saying, "The real danger is of coming to believe such dreadful things about Him. The conclusion I dread is not, 'So there's no God after all,' but 'so that is what God's really like. Deceive yourself no longer.'"[10] That is why we must turn to the objective Word of God in determining who He really is.

What does the world need? Someone to fix a big problem here and there, or does it need a Savior? Dorothée Soelle made an important observation when she said, "The faith that disintegrates in experience is a theism that has almost nothing to do with Christ."[11] In many determinations about God, Jesus Christ receives little mention or consideration. Later in this book, we will be looking at why Christ makes a crucial difference in how we perceive and deal with the state of the world.

People throughout history have encountered God in various ways and have given descriptions of their experiences. However, it is important to point out two complementary truths. First, we do not know God *without* experience. Second, we do not know God *only by* experience. The questions of the heart demand response. I use the word *response* because *answer* corresponds more to the realm of law or logic, and we need something that satisfies our hearts and minds.

GIVE ME SOMETHING TO STAND ON

Well-meaning people often give feel-good answers to the hard questions of life, but when one experiences the depths of suffering and brokenness, the activities of the outside world can seem superficial. I know I have never wanted simplistic or trite reasoning. Such pat answers make the inquirer think, "This person doesn't really care or understand. They just think they have to say something." Religious people especially feel they are expected to have the answers to life's most vexing questions, so they tend to offer pious-sounding, untested clichés, which hold little value in the face of pain.

Suffering reduces one's tolerance for superficiality.

Emphases on appearances, pleasure, and external perfor-
mance are offensive, if not repulsive. Jesus linked hypocrisy
with superficiality. When shallowness infects religion, the
effects can be devastating to those who suffer. People who
know they are hurting may seek a doctor or some sort of
counselor. But if the doctors and counselors of this world are
not able to offer concrete answers with eternal value, the
wounded are left wondering where else to turn for help.

Hypocrisy is present within Christendom (both evangeli-
cal and non-evangelical) as well as in all of the religions of the
world. When elements such as sentimental frivolity, entertainment, and a good laugh replace the search for God, devo-
tion to Him, and love for one another, all we are left with is
fluffy cotton candy rather than sustaining nourishment.

A correct knowledge of the reality of God is necessary to
live in accordance with His will. It is important that we heed
the caution to avoid making God to be what we want Him to
be (see, for example, Romans 1:23, 25). After his wife's tragic
death, C. S. Lewis admitted, "Images of the Holy easily become holy images—sacrosanct. My idea of God is not a divine idea. It has to be shattered time after time. He shatters it
Himself. He is the great iconoclast. . . . All reality is icono-
clastic."[12] Indeed, when our icons (or anything we cling to
for security) are broken by reality, our security systems are
fractured. We are plunged into an inward suffering that is in
many ways inexplicable, and even if communicated, would
be misunderstood by many. The ultimate questions will
surge to the surface of our hearts and minds.

And this questioning is not a bad thing. It is not by hold-
ing on to our comfortable notions of God and of our simplistic explanations of the difficulties of life that we mature. It is
by the continuous questioning and forming and re-forming
of our beliefs—even the shattering of them—that our under-

standing begins to contain substance rather than trite, pat answers. Perhaps the most comforting and intriguing response is to admit there are many things we just do not understand.

The issue of the existence and relevance of God will normally surface in times of trouble. It is the most fundamental question of all, since the meaning of our existence is tied to His existence. A person in crisis may cry out the briefest prayer of all: "O God!" Many people say they believe in the concept of prayer. Many testify that they experience the presence of God in their most difficult times. And in the Bible's most penetrating examination of suffering, the patriarch Job discovered that profound pain can lead to a direct encounter with the living God.

SEARCHING FOR
UNDERSTANDING IN JOB'S ORDEAL

In the beginning of Job's story, we are given a glimpse of the workings behind the scenes when Satan asks God's permission to test Job. The rest of the book of Job is devoted to finding the reason behind his devastating suffering. From the outset of the account, he loses virtually everything, and in the aftermath he and his companions sit silently in grief.

After he and his friends spend considerable time and effort in trying to make sense of what had happened to Job, God appears from the darkness and confronts Job, directing him to consider the wonders of creation. Through understanding God's power as the giver of all life, Job begins to understand God's working in his own life. Job boldly had protested to God the tragic things that had come upon him. When God replied, He asked Job, "Where were you when I laid the earth's foundation?" (Job 38:4) and He goes on throughout the rest of chapters 38 and 39 asking Job if he can explain the wonders of God's creation.

As he heard the voice of God and marveled at His working, he was quieted and humbled.

> I know that you can do all things; no plan of yours can be thwarted. You asked, "Who is this that obscures my knowledge? Surely I spoke of things I did not understand, things too wonderful for me to know."
>
> —Job 42:1–4

Though it may seem strange, it is vital for every sufferer to come to a true humility. It is the broken, humbled heart, which can begin to receive answers to its cries.

We can learn much from Job. When it comes to confronting the problem of evil, we need a vision of the Holy One—more than answers, philosophical discussions, or superficial religious talk. God never really gave Job answers as to why he experienced such great suffering. Perhaps he didn't need to know, but what we do need to know is the true essence of the nature of God. This God is not a secret enemy, as Job once implied, but One who comes down, is good, true, righteous, and a gracious Friend.[13] God's response to Job was personal. He spoke to Job directly because He is in the business of relationship. Job needed to hear the voice of God more than he needed all the answers to his questions about suffering, and more than he needed an end to the suffering itself. Consistent with His personal revelation to all mankind over time, God revealed a divine approach in addressing Job's ordeal. God ultimately dealt with him *personally* rather than providing a comprehensive explanation of global suffering.

As the Almighty responded to His servant Job, He painted a much bigger picture than Job had ever seen. Job concludes,

"My ears had heard of you but now my eyes have seen you" (Job 42:5). Instead of receiving a limited, incomplete answer, Job encountered the very person of God.

THE MYSTERIOUS GOD

So who is this God who revealed Himself to Job and wants to reveal Himself to us? We'll dive into that in the next chapter, because God's revelation of Himself is a better guide through life than experience alone. And we'll need His help since there will always be suffering and the enemy of death in this fallen world. "The last enemy to be destroyed is death" (1 Corinthians 15:26; also see verses 54, 55).

Though it is our nature to want all the answers, we do not have the moral, intellectual, or spiritual capabilities to explain all of God's designs and acts (see Romans 11:33–36). Could you or I answer the questions about the universe that God posed to Job? No, not even the world's greatest scientists can figure it all out. When God asked Job to explain the inner workings of the universe, Job could only respond with silence. If God's creation is a marvel, how much more complex are God's designs and plans for men?

The greatness and mystery of God must humble us. As Philip Yancey observed in his book *Rumors of Another World,* it's hard to be a creature unable to comprehend his Creator:

> Accepting creatureliness may require that I, like Job, bow before a master plan that makes no apparent sense. In the face of doubt, I have learned the simple response of considering the alternatives. If there is no Creator, what then? I would have to view the world with all its suffering as well as all its beauty as a random product of a meaningless universe, the briefest flare of a match in cosmic darkness. Perhaps the very sense

that *something is wrong* is itself a rumor of transcendence, an inbuilt longing for a healed planet on which God's will is done on earth as it is in heaven.[14]

When we come to things we are not able to understand completely, we find the matter of faith at the core of human life. Ultimately, every person has to decide where he or she will place trust: in oneself—one's character, intentions, abilities? or in a mysterious God who will reveal Himself fully, though gradually?

We receive what might be called "divine impressions" from God, but such are hard to express in human terminology to the satisfaction of a philosopher. As Pascal pointed out, "Either God is or he is not. But to which view shall we be inclined? Reason cannot decide this question."[15] We must either accept the reality of the living God and reach out to Him, or we can deny the reality of God. If we make the latter choice, we have made the choice to believe in self and nothing else. With this sort of escapism, people seek to remain in their old, familiar surroundings, the shelter of straw, which did not stand the storms in the first place. As stated previously, they become what M. Scott Peck called, "people of the lie."[16] Yet they deny or ignore their greatest inner need and its remedy that was placarded before them in their time of suffering. It is what Pascal called the "infinite abyss [that] can be filled only with an infinite and immutable object; in other words by God Himself."[17] But where do we *find* God? In our rationalistic and technological age, many have deluded themselves into thinking that we will be able to see everything tangibly with a microscope, telescope, or some other mechanism. Yet we believe in many things that are not visible to the human eye—gravity, energy, the relationship between one's body and spirit, and love in relationship, for example. We know these things are real because we can see their results, but we cannot experience them with our physical senses.

Perhaps love is the best example of a well-known force unexplainable by the natural sciences. Love is not always reasonable—and certainly not unconditional love. Godly parents, friends, and spouses know that showing love is often *not* logical in the face of another's actions. Love is given, not because the recipient deserves it but because love exists in the giver. When we give or receive such love, we have a picture of God's love, which defies reason. And we cannot *know* we are loved without the heart being involved.

In the Bible we find a divine invitation to engage our hearts: "You will seek me and find me when you seek me with all your heart" (Jeremiah 29:13). "Seek the LORD while he may be found; call on him while he is near" (Isaiah 55:6). However, from the outset of our journey we have to check our expectations at the door. God's revelation of Himself will be different than we expect, not matching our preconceived notions and images. The question is, will we still want Him? Do we want God as He reveals Himself? Or do we insist on retaining our idea of God? Remember what C. S. Lewis has said: "The conclusion I dread is not, 'So there's no God after all,' but 'so that is what God's really like. Deceive yourself no longer.'"[18] A decision has to be made between courageously pursuing truth and clinging to our notions, to what may even turn out to be fantasy. As any parent or person who has had a disciplining parent knows, truth is hard to swallow sometimes. Nonetheless we are the better for it.

There are truths about God, humankind, and the seasons of life that we can know and take comfort in, here and now. Wherever you are in your pursuit of truth, I invite you to come along with me as we move from experiential limitations to dig into what answers God has given us.

I am God, and there is no other;
I am God, and there is none like me.
I make known the end from the beginning,
From ancient times, what is still to come.
I say: My purpose will stand,
And I will do all that I please. . . .
What I have said, that will I bring about;
What I have planned, that will I do.
I am he; I am the first and I am the last.
                    —Isaiah 46:9–11; 48:12

QUESTIONS
FOR REFLECTION

1. What is the "integrity of suffering"? Is it our human nature to try to find meaning in crisis? Or do we tend to gloss over the reality of crisis? According to the author, what are the causes and effects of our tendency to "suppress the reality of suffering"?

2. What are some of the different categories of crisis people experience?

3. Read Romans 1:23, 25. In what ways do we tend to make God what we want Him to be? Do you agree with the author that we have to "check our expectations (of God) at the door"? Comment on what C. S. Lewis said: "The conclusion I dread is not 'So there's no God after all,' but 'so that is what God's really like. Deceive yourself no longer.'"

4. Describe a time you experienced a crisis and a friend reacted by saying, "Everything's fine" or "You've got it made, compared to so-and-so."

*"One thing God has spoken,
two things have I heard:
that you, O God, are strong,
and that you, O Lord, are loving."*

WHO IS THE SOVEREIGN GOD? A VERY PRESENT POWER

WE'VE MENTIONED the insightful story Jesus told about two home builders. One builder built his house on a rock. Storms came, and the rain poured down in torrents. The floodwaters were like large rolling waves in an out-of-control ocean, and the wind blew furiously and beat on the house. There was an ominous darkness punctured only by fierce streaks of lightning and loud explosions of thunder. Yet the house did not collapse. Another man built a house and experienced the same type of storm. His house collapsed with a mighty crash and was washed away into oblivion. The difference between the two houses was that one was built on rock and the other was built on sand. These houses represent the foundations of people's lives. If your life is not built on the rock, it will come apart in the pressure of the storm.

The storms of life expose the stuff we are made of by removing the superficial ornamentation in our lives. When the external props of existence—possessions, appearances, and the things valued by the world—are stripped away, we are left with only the core of our hearts and souls. We discover what we truly know and believe about this life and the Creator.

Suffering can lead us to an encounter with God. Oftentimes, He will be the rock that keeps us from being blown apart by the fiercest storms of all. Some who suffer will change their view of God—for better or for worse. For example, Harold Kushner, in his book *When Bad Things Happen to Good People*, developed a view of a God who does not have power to intervene and keep bad things from happening. This is, in many respects, an impotent God.

It is not sufficient to simply believe in God's existence, just as it is not sufficient for a builder to simply believe that a strong foundation is better than a weak foundation. The strong foundation must actually be built and put in place; it must be established, not merely approved on a blueprint or in the mind.

How Can We Know God?

We actually have an invitation from God Himself to know Him: "Let not the wise man boast of his wisdom or the strong man boast of his strength or the rich man boast of his riches, but let him who boasts boast about this: that he understands and knows me" (Jeremiah 9:23–24).

God states in no uncertain terms that knowing Him is of the utmost value; it is He Himself who initiates a relationship with mankind, and He Himself who invites us to search for truth. He has not made Himself secretive—He has, in fact, revealed Himself in several ways: through His dialogue with His chosen people of Israel, through His Son who became flesh, through the revelation of the Scriptures, and through the Holy Spirit who guides us into truth.

Since my college days, my focus has been the search for truth. My search led me to begin the quest for truth by accepting that the Bible is what it claims to be—the self-revelation of the living God. It is in the Bible, then, that we find light to guide us through this unmapped darkness. The search for the truth about God and His plans does not make for an easy journey, but we can take comfort that the process will not lead to a dead end either.

Where do we start in understanding the reality of God? Not everyone, obviously, accepts the Bible as God's revealed truth, but the Bible itself says there is a knowledge of something beyond the tangible world that is engraved on our hearts and minds. "He has also set eternity in the hearts of men" (Ecclesiastes 3:11). God Himself has built the search for and awareness of that which is beyond the visible into our consciousness. Apart from His written Word, therefore, God has left at least two kinds of evidence about Himself. They are (1) His eternal *power*, as is apparent in creation, and (2) His divine *nature* (Romans 1:19–20).

Only a divine being is capable of creating a world like ours and having a plan to redeem it from its chosen sinfulness. God alone could speak with total accuracy to the prophets and writers of Scripture and tell them the things to come—and then cause those events to come to pass. They point directly to the reality that He is the sovereign, living God. The recognition of this brings about worship of Him and allows us to focus on His presence and power in this world. When we have a sufficient understanding of who God is, we can begin to form a proper perspective on everything in the world, suffering included.

HE IS ETERNAL

Eternally present and existent, the Creator has neither beginning nor end. The entire universe is composed of time and space and matter and energy. All things interact with and are limited by these attributes, and they all head toward entropy and death. But God, being separate from the universe and superior to the creation, is not bound by time or space, and is not composed of matter or energy. He is eternal, unrestricted by the limits of creation.

God's eternal nature was affirmed by Abraham, Moses, John, Paul, Peter, and many of the other writers of Scripture. As Moses said, "Before the mountains were born or you brought forth the earth and the world, from everlasting to everlasting you are God" (Psalm 90:2). Every one of the attributes of the living God can be described as eternal—eternal love, eternal justice, and eternal holiness.

HE IS INVOLVED

God is omnipresent—always present. This aspect of the character of God is fundamental to an understanding of Him. His omnipresence allows Him ultimate access to all humanity. Restricted by neither time nor space, the Creator is in constant contact with each aspect of His creation. He does not have to make appointments and decide who has His counsel first because He can listen to all of us at the same time.

Some, however, hold to and even prefer the idea of a God who can be compared to a watchmaker. This view, known as deism, sees God as making the watch (creation) and then setting it aside to run by itself. This God exists, but is uninterested in the affairs of the world. He is impersonal.

He created the world, but then removed Himself from an active role and left mankind alone.[19]

But such a view is far from the truth. Consider what God Himself has said:

> The eyes of the LORD are everywhere, keeping
> watch on the wicked and the good.
> —Proverbs 15:3

> For the eyes of the LORD range throughout the
> earth to strengthen those whose hearts are fully
> committed to him.
> —2 Chronicles 16:9

> For this is what the high and lofty One says—he who lives
> forever, whose name is holy: "I live in a high and holy place,
> but also with him who is contrite and lowly in spirit, to revive
> the spirit of the lowly and to revive the heart of the contrite."
> —Isaiah 57:15

> He does not take his eyes off the righteous.
> —Job 36:7

From His own account then, as recorded in the Bible, is what God wants us to know about Himself—and it is evident that God is present and active. He always takes the first step in forging relationships and has been relating to people on a personal level since the creation of Adam and Eve. God initiated the perfect relationship with our first parents back in the beginning of His relationship with mankind, and then initiated the necessary steps to provide for a restoration after their disobedience caused their relationship with Him to be broken.

As we recount the narratives that occurred after Adam

and Eve's time, we see God still very much involved in the lives of such people as Noah, Abraham, Isaac, Jacob, Joseph. For hundreds and thousands of years after creating the first humans, we clearly see God continuing to be a part of the lives of those He has created. God went on to reveal His unique qualities to His chosen people, Israel, through the patriarch Moses. God made it explicitly clear that He was unlike any of the false gods of Egypt, which were only copies of things on earth. Moses told the Israelites, "Know therefore today, and take it to your heart, that the Lord, He is God in heaven above and on the earth below; there is no other" (Deuteronomy 4:39 NASB). Through the trials of their slavery in Egypt, their escape, and then the long years of wandering in the desert, God taught Israel that He was always with them.

Hundreds of years later, the psalmist asks: "Where can I go from your Spirit? Where can I flee from your presence? If I go up to the heavens, you are there; If I make my bed in the depths, you are there" (Psalm 139:7–8).

Still later, the prophet Jeremiah reported the words of God: "'Am I a God who is near,' declares the Lord, 'And not a God far off? Can a man hide himself in hiding places so I do not see him?' declares the Lord. 'Do I not fill the heavens and the earth?'" (Jeremiah 23:23–24 NASB).

NOTHING IS HIDDEN

Intimately related to the dynamic presence of the living God is His complete knowledge. The omniscience of God points to the reality that He knows all. Omniscience means He is constantly aware of all that is taking place and nothing is hidden from Him. One of the classic statements on the knowledge of God is found in an awesome psalm that had a

deep impact on my wife and me when we suffered the loss of
our one-month-old son:

> O LORD, you have searched me and you know me.
> You know when I sit and when I rise;
> You perceive my thoughts from afar.
> You discern my going out and my lying down;
> You are familiar with all my ways.
> Before a word is on my tongue you know it completely,
>   O LORD . . .
> My frame was not hidden from you when I was made in the
>   secret place.
> When I was woven together in the depths of the earth, your
>   eyes saw my unformed body.
> All the days ordained for me were written in your book
>   before one of them came to be.
> —Psalm 139:1–4, 15–16

God's awareness of the events of the universe is much
more than just a general supervision. It is a profound knowledge of every specific act and even thought. "Nothing in all
creation is hidden from God's sight. Everything is uncov-
ered and laid bare before the eyes of him to whom we must
give account" (Hebrews 4:13; also see Jeremiah 16:17).

The Creator's understanding pierces the external, allow-
ing Him a full view of the thoughts and intentions of man.
"Man looks at the outward appearance, but the LORD looks
at the heart" (1 Samuel 16:7). "[Jesus] knew what was in a
man" (John 2:25). God is concerned with our hearts and not
our external appearance or accomplishments. That should
not surprise us, because God is spirit (John 4:24). Therefore,
He is concerned first of all with the spiritual—the heart.

Believing that God sees and knows what we are going

through is extremely important in times of trouble. A woman named Hagar found herself the victim of harsh treatment by her mistress, Sarah. Due to the severe indignities and suffering to which she was subjected, Hagar, who was pregnant at the time, fled into the desert wilderness. As she trekked through the desert alone, feeling rejected and despised, pregnant and totally vulnerable, she came to a spring of water. God (identified as the "angel of the LORD") appeared to her and placed a blessing on her unborn son. The name of the boy is to be Ishmael, He says, because "the Lord has given heed to your affliction" (Genesis 16:11 NASB). In response Hagar says, "You are the God who sees me" (verse 13). The place where she was came to be called Beer Lahai Roi, "a well of the living One who sees me."

This suffering woman experienced the presence of the living God. She met Him who not only sees and knows, but also involves Himself in people's lives in an active manner. For those facing catastrophe, the world can seem to enclose into a small, painful capsule of existence dominated by pain. But when God's children call upon their listening Father, "God himself sets their faces in the right direction."[20] The light of His self-revelation knocks down the walls of that imprisoning world of suffering and reveals the dawning of a new day.

The personal, active presence of the living God was known to Abraham, Isaac, Jacob, Joshua, Hannah, David, Mary, Peter, Paul, and many more. As David wrote, "The LORD is near to all who call on him, to all who call on him in truth" (Psalm 145:18). This is why we hear a frequent refrain throughout Scripture: "Do not fear. I am with you." (Some of these Scriptures are Deuteronomy 1:21; Joshua 1:9; and Isaiah 41:10.) This is not a threat, that He's looking to find fault; but knowing that God is always present and knows all becomes an anchor for the soul.

HE IS CONCERNED

Another common metaphor for this caring, constant omnipresence of the Lord is that of a shepherd. This reality has warmed the hearts of those who know God. Jacob referred to "the God who has been my shepherd all my life to this day" (Genesis 48:15). "The LORD is my shepherd . . . even though I walk through the valley of the shadow of death, I will fear no evil, for you are with me, " David proclaimed in Psalm 23. This same God says, "Never will I leave you; never will I forsake you" (Hebrews 13:5). Jesus Christ Himself said, "And surely I am with you always, to the very end of the age" (Matthew 28:20).

THE ULTIMATE GOOD

How does His eternality, His omnipresence, and His concern matter in our lives? When He is declared to be the living God in the Bible, He is revealed as the active God who can intervene and deliver people from suffering. According to His wisdom and timing, He will respond to our troubles in one way or another. He knows when and how to bring good into our lives. Does this mean He will spare us from pain and depression? No, obviously not. But suffering can lead us closer to God, as was the case with Job and so many others. But God is interested in our ultimate and eternal glory, and this brings us to an important conclusion.

Our *ultimate* good is this: being transformed into the likeness of Christ. "And we, who with unveiled faces all reflect the Lord's glory, are being transformed into his likeness with ever-increasing glory, which comes from the Lord, who is the Spirit" (2 Corinthians 3:18). This process takes place throughout our lives.

When our lives on earth come to an end and as believers see Christ, "we shall be like him, for we shall see him as he is" (1 John 3:2). Only by exiting this life can we reach our final destination and true home since we are "aliens and strangers" in this world (1 Peter 2:11). God's love for us is displayed through His immense interest in our present and eternal spiritual condition. He has done, and will do, everything necessary to bring us into a deeper relationship with Him now on earth, and eventually will bring us into His presence when we leave the confines of our earthly life. Everything else is peripheral.

The Creator takes us through the tribulations of this life and also takes us through the end of this life at death. In our fallen world, we cannot expect to be immune from difficulty. But because He who has conquered death is with us, we have nothing to fear since our hope is in Him. Through Christ's death, all gaps between God and man have been bridged. We can be fully confident in His final victory over all things. Remarkably, even before His death on the cross, Jesus said, "In this world you will have trouble. But take heart! I have overcome the world" (John 16:33).

HE IS OMNIPOTENT

As the Creator who formed everything from nothing, God's awesome power is beyond our comprehension. His mastery of every aspect of our complex universe hints at His might and strength.

The psalmist David said, "One thing God has spoken, two things have I heard: that you, O God, are strong, and that you, O Lord, are loving" (Psalm 62:11–12). These two attributes of God, His power and love, are twin pillars that support the universe.

Whether in creation or miracles in this world, the pictures painted of this divine power in numerous biblical accounts are impressive. To express the concept of the sovereignty of God, the writers of Scripture used terms related to royalty and majesty such as King, Lord, and Master. Paul described God as, "The King eternal, immortal, invisible, the only God. . . . God, the blessed and only Ruler, the King of kings and Lord of lords, who alone is immortal and who lives in unapproachable light" (1 Timothy 1:17; 6:15–16).

Omnipotence is so central to the character of God that it might be called the compendium, or summary, of all other attributes, which is why the early church felt it was accurate to describe God with this one attribute in their creeds.[21] Deity and power are both unlimited and inseparable. As we seek to understand and know God, the terms *omnipotence* and *rule* are often used interchangeably.

The sovereignty of God is based upon His power. This power, His omnipotence, is at the core of who He is—His person. This matter of the power of God is comforting and exciting because He is not like us. Things are never out of control to Him. He has power in all realms whether it be our physical bodies, the world of creation, or our hearts.

This power over our physical bodies is exemplified miraculously in the case of Sarah, Abraham's wife. She had suffered from her inability to have children for years, a great grief for a woman in the ancient world. God said she would have a child in her old age, demonstrating that nothing is impossible for Him (Genesis 18:14). This power is beyond our comprehension as the Scripture describes Him as being able to "do immeasurably more than all we ask or imagine, according to his power that is at work within us" (Ephesians 3:20).

Because the creation exemplifies and reveals God's attributes, many people, regardless of their religious beliefs, experience a measure of emotional healing by contemplating the wonders of the universe. This also explains why many religions emphasize some aspect of nature as part of their spiritual focus.

The power and splendor of creation *are* therapeutic. Many suffering people find a quiet remedy in nature's glory because the complexity and beauty of the earth point to the power of the Creator. These works of God "declare the glory of God," specifically His great power and wisdom (Psalm 19:1). Remember that God told Job to examine several aspects of His creation as part of His self-revelation (Job 38–41).

THE RIGHTFUL KING

In *Return of the King*, the last book of the J. R. R. Tolkien saga The Lord of the Rings, we see the hailing of a king. Up until this point, the members of the "fellowship of the ring" had been immersed in the worst possible battles—against the evil inside the souls of men and beasts, and the source of Evil itself (in this saga, the Eye of Sauron). A glimpse of the scene as Middle Earth received Aragorn as king:

> Then Frodo came forward and took the crown from Faramir and bore it to Gandalf; and Aragorn knelt, and Gandalf set the White Crown upon his head, and said: "Now come the days of the King, and may they be blessed while the thrones of the Valar endure!"
>
> But when Aragorn arose all that beheld him gazed in silence, for it seemed to them that he was revealed to them now for the first time. Tall as the sea-kings of old he stood above all that were near; ancient of days he seemed and yet in the flower of manhood; and wisdom sat upon his brow, and

strength and healing were in his hands, and a light was about him. And then Faramir cried: "Behold the King!"

And in that moment all the trumpets were blown. . . . In this time the City was made more fair than it had ever been, even in the days of its first glory.[22]

The royal majesty of God is depicted throughout the Bible. It is said that the Almighty is seated on a throne, high and exalted, His glory filling the temple (Isaiah 6:1; also see 2 Chronicles 18:18; Acts 7:55–56; Revelation 4:1–11). Picture that throne with all the majesty and aura of the divine King in all of His glory. Anyone who has only a brief glimpse of the glory of the Great King will bow down and worship, as was often the case in recorded visions of God.

Since God created and owns all things, He has the right to rule and determine the outcome of all creation. In the prophecy of Jeremiah, we see that God's authority is like the right the potter has over the clay: " 'Can I not do with you as this potter does?' declares the LORD. 'Like clay in the hand of the potter, so are you in my hand' " (Jeremiah 18:6).

God's rule is a benevolent, divine dominion. His power becomes the expression of His wisdom, righteousness, goodness, and love. The power of God is yoked with the wisdom of God, and all creation carries His unique stamp. In Proverbs 8:22–31, we see wisdom personified, talking about the Lord and her [wisdom's] eternal presence:

> "The LORD brought me [wisdom] forth as the first of his works, before his deeds of old; I was appointed from eternity, from the beginning, before the world began. When there were no oceans, I was given birth, when there were no springs abounding with water; before the mountains were settled in place, before the hills, I was given birth, before he made the

earth or its fields or any of the dust of the world. I was there when he set the heavens in place, when he marked out the horizon on the face of the deep, when he established the clouds above and fixed securely the fountains of the deep, when he gave the sea its boundary so the waters would not overstep his command, and when he marked out the foundations of the earth. Then I was the craftsman at his side. I was filled with delight day after day, rejoicing always in his presence, rejoicing in his whole world and delighting in mankind."

We can trust our wise King, who knew how to put the entire universe together, to know what we need and how to meet those needs in His timing.

The success of any kingdom is dependent upon the nature of the king. As a perfect King, God's kingdom reflects His attributes. As we align our desires with the desires of the King, we experience a profound unity with our Creator. When Jesus teaches His disciples how to pray, He indicates that God's kingdom is joined to following His will. "Your kingdom come, your will be done on earth as it is in heaven" (Matthew 6:10). We usually recite these words, pausing after "your will be done." But consider what it means to pray, "Your will be done on earth"—just the way it's already being carried out in heaven. When we follow and live out His will on earth, we are imitating the operation of His kingdom in heaven. Though this world has been influenced by Satan ever since the fall, as we live in harmony with God's will, we bring a part of His kingdom to this life.

The Bible also tells us that this imperfect world will not last forever; the King will have a wholly perfect kingdom, ushered in by "loud voices of heaven, which [say]: 'The kingdom of the world has become the kingdom of our Lord and of his Christ, and he will reign for ever and ever' "(Revelation 11:15).

HOLINESS IN EFFECT

The sovereign God is holy, literally meaning "set apart." In fact, the title "Holy One" is one of the names for God (Isaiah 43:14–15). Holiness, a relational term, defines who God is in relationship to man and the created things. His holiness can be described in three parts.

First, as a Being totally free and unencumbered by any constraints, God is holy in that He is *incomparable* to anything else because He created all things. As the Lord's Prayer helps us remember this uniqueness: "Hallowed be your name" (Matthew 6:9), that is, "May Your name [You] be recognized as holy."

The second part receives the greatest emphasis in the Bible. That is, God is *separate from sin* and all moral impurity. Holiness in this sense emphasizes the total perfection of the living God. Evil will be annihilated by the Holy One. This part of holiness is uncomfortable for us. As David Wells has said in his book *God in the Wasteland*, "God in his holiness is deeply and irrevocably set in opposition to the world because of its sin. . . . Until we recognize the holiness of God, our religion will be merely superficial, a play thing designed by consumers who are used to getting what they want the way they want it."[23] God charges us, "Be holy, because I, the LORD your God, am holy" (Leviticus 19:2; see 1 Peter 1:15–16).

This brings us to the third characteristic of true holiness. This could be called dynamic holiness. You and I cannot encounter this holiness without being affected. It possesses an unmistakable attraction as we come to yearn to be like Him. This kind of holiness usually receives the least attention. As

Rudolf Otto described in his fine book *The Idea of the Holy*, it is the numinous, mysterious, suprarational power that *transforms us.*[24]

God's holiness, power, and love are united and interdependent.

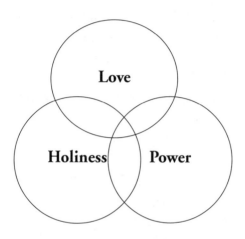

HE IS RIGHTEOUS

In prayer, Jesus Christ identified God the Father as both "Holy Father" and "Righteous Father" (John 17:11, 25). His righteousness and His rule are inseparable. Our great King expressed His authority by establishing laws and the framework for justice and peace. His directions for living—called *Torah*, meaning "instruction"—are a reflection of His holiness. Man can rebel as much as he desires, but evidence for the authority and rule of God is written on the hearts of all mankind as explained in Romans 2:15.

Not only is God the Lawgiver, but He is also the "Judge of all the earth" (Genesis 18:25). It is the responsibility of the great King to rule with righteousness and justice. This is nowhere clearer than in the Old Testament Scriptures, which lay the foundation for the New Testament revelation. Many things take place in this world and in our personal lives that are hard to reconcile with justice and righteousness. They are not in line with our definition of what is fair. We, however, have a limited perspective compared to the eternal, timeless understanding of the working of God.

The biblical word for *righteousness* indicates a standard to be met. Just as there are standard weights and measures in the material world, God sets the benchmark in the spiritual realm. As God Himself is pure holiness, so He is the absolute standard for righteousness and justice. From the very beginning we see the living God, the great King, described unequivocally by Moses in the following: "He is the Rock, his works are perfect, and all his ways are just. A faithful God who does no wrong, 'upright and just is he' " (Deuteronomy 32:4). Notice the words of a great worship psalm:

The LORD reigns, let the earth be glad;
Let the distant shores rejoice.
Clouds and thick darkness surround him;
Righteousness and justice are the foundation of his throne.
Fire goes before him
And consumes his foes on every side. . . .
The heavens proclaim his righteousness.
                                                    —Psalm 97:1–3, 6

As we see from the description of God consuming His foes, righteousness involves the workings of justice. This fact should cause the evildoer to tremble before the Lord, the all-knowing Judge. And it should give comfort to the weak, because the righteous God cares about the vulnerable, like widows and orphans, for He is "a father to the fatherless, a defender of widows" (Psalm 68:5; also see Deuteronomy 10:17–18).

Just as a child can roam free and safe in the protective boundaries and rules of his parents, righteousness and justice lead to peace. The Hebrew word for peace, *shalom*, means not only the absence of conflict but also "health" and the "good life." Being part of the family of God leads to this *shalom*, where "righteousness and peace kiss each other" (Psalm 85:10).

God has provided the way for us to be righteous—and it is not by perfectly obeying the law. Our righteousness, in a biblical sense, is focused on acceptance by God. This is only possible by receiving the gift of Christ's righteousness by faith. In chapter 4 we will be looking at how the life, death, and resurrection of Jesus paved the way for triumph over suffering and pain, making provision for perfect, eternal peace.

UNREASONABLE LOVE

Not only is He the Almighty, the Holy One, the righteous King, but He is also good. "The LORD is righteous in all his ways and loving toward all he has made" (Psalm 145:17). Love and goodness are the headwaters from which flow all of His gifts to humanity. He is unique in this pure goodness as Jesus Christ said, "No one is good—except God alone" (Luke 18:19). Hear the refrain of the songs of praise:

> The LORD is good to all;
> he has compassion on all he has made. . . .
> For the LORD is good and his love endures forever;
> his faithfulness continues through all generations.
> —Psalms 145:9; 100:5

In His actions, God is tenderhearted, compassionate, generous, merciful, and full of grace. He is the giver of every "good and perfect gift" (James 1:17). Theologian A. W. Tozer pointed out that while our actions don't always merit God's kindness, even still God is often "inclined to bestow blessedness" upon us, taking "holy pleasure in the happiness of His people."[25] It is His love that will draw us to Him because, "we love because he first loved us" (1 John 4:19).

The greatest demonstration of divine goodness is seen in the relationship God has with those He has bound to Himself in relationship. Here, the outpouring of divine love, mercy, and grace is immense and incomparably beautiful. One of the simple statements about this all-encompassing attribute of God is "God is love" (1 John 4:16). "The love of a holy God to sinners is the most mysterious attribute of the divine nature."[26] Ultimately it is the *sacrificial love* of God that will provide the only real answer to a fallen world, which we discuss in the next chapter.

PROVIDENTIAL DESIGN

Looking at history can help us learn about God's providence. Not only do we gain perspective on the past, but we gain a view of the future through looking at the history of providence. Bringing the past and the future together, we can see that there is a design to it all—what philosophers call a metanarrative. "A metanarrative is a grand overarching account, or all-encompassing story, which is thought to give order to the historical record."[27] The Bible is the greatest source to get insight into God's comprehensive plan. Solomon spoke of God's providence and our desire to seek it out: "He [God] has made everything beautiful in its time. He has also set eternity in the hearts of men; yet they cannot fathom what God has done from beginning to end" (Ecclesiastes 3:11). One contemporary translation says it this way: "He has given us a desire to know the future, but never gives us the satisfaction of fully understanding what he does" (TEV).

There are obvious signs of design, direction, and movement in the universe. They are like gleams of a pearl buried deep within the shell of an oyster. Slowly the pearl becomes visible—first in outline form, then in its glory as more and more of it is exposed. Its brilliance and luster are only seen in the presence of light. Likewise, when a person begins to understand the reality of providence as the active involvement of God, they see the unveiling of His person. His attributes of holiness, goodness and love, righteousness and justice, and His great power are all manifested in perfect combination and symmetry.

History is being played out according to God's design and direction. This fact is of the utmost importance. Some may have an adverse reaction to such truth because of the apparent unfairness in life. It is not hard to come up with experiences that cause us to question life as we know it. But if we truly know God personally, our outlook is different because we come from the perspective of relationship rather than a skeptic. We find His promise of Romans 8:28 to be ultimate reality: "And we know that in all things God works for the good of those who love him, who have been called according to his purpose."

AN INVITATION TO
TRUST IN HIS PROVIDENCE

When I left home for the first time and traveled hundreds of miles away from my family, I experienced loneliness and fear. I will never forget one certain night when I was traveling and had stopped at a motel. In the drawer I found a Bible. I didn't know where to turn for help, but as I randomly

opened the Bible some powerful words met my eyes. Those
words changed my life. "The LORD is my light and my
salvation—whom shall I fear? The LORD is the stronghold
of my life—of whom shall I be afraid?" (Psalm 27:1).

In light of the sovereignty of God I now recognize three
things: (1) I'm not in control, (2) things really aren't out of
control, and (3) He is in control. Though we might not be
aware of it, one of the major issues we wrestle with in suffering is the matter of control—control of our lives, control of
the future, control of the situation, and so on. When suffering has done its teaching, the issue of control is settled. At
that point the heart recognizes that the Lord has the ultimate
authority and power.

A certain description of providence takes precedence in
my mind. After my wife's death, my sons and I moved from
Phoenix back to the Midwest. The changes kept coming
like a deluge. As I was unpacking boxes, I found a soap dish
made by one of my wife's friends. I noticed a stone embedded
in the glossy dish. The following words were artistically
painted on it, "God won't send us where he is unable to sustain us." That's providence. I've read those words again
and again in midst of dark days and multiple adjustments. It
just goes to show that great statements of faith can be found
in simple words like those in Psalm 31:14–15: "But I trust in
you, O LORD; I say, 'You are my God.' My times are in
your hands."

When one comes to the recognition of God's providence, a decision of faith is necessary. If I do not surrender
and submit to His sovereignty, I plunge myself deeper into
despair. Turning to Him in humble submission is the gateway to the future of a life more fully in harmony with His
ways. This is not simple, and it does not happen overnight. It
is a matter of trusting, of pressing on, and of maturing. Jesus

said, "If you hold to my teaching, you are really my disciples. Then you will know the truth, and the truth will set you free" (John 8:31–32). Knowledge of the truth leads to freedom from worry, from slavery to sin, from wondering what the point of life is—which Jesus also made clear to us: "This is eternal life: that they may know you, the only true God, and Jesus Christ, whom you have sent" (John 17:3). In Him there is relief, release, renewal, and even rejoicing.

It comes down to believing that He has—and has always had—a plan. Providence includes everything that happens now, has ever happened, or will happen in the future—down to the minutest detail. God has knowledge of the future and what is needed, from the basic provisions for sustaining life to the most inner spiritual needs of man.

The profound phrases found in Psalm 145:13–21 illustrate this truth. "The LORD is faithful to all his promises and loving toward all he has made." "You give them their food at the proper time." "The LORD is near to all who call on him." "The LORD watches over all who love him." Though a simplistic analogy in comparison, this type of providence is similar to how every parent is involved with provision for the future as they care for their children.

Providence can be defined as the constant working of the guiding and sustaining hand of God in all things according to His intended purposes and design. It is God's personal and active involvement in all things that take place, everywhere and at all times.

A verse in the book of Job gives this truth in capsule form: "In his hand is the life of every creature and the breath of all mankind" (Job 12:10).

THE USE OF EVIL

We cannot leave the discussion of God's attributes including His providence without facing some difficult questions: *Does God use evil? How can He use evil? Is He doing evil?*

Scholar Meir Sternberg points out that the narratives of the Bible inculcate "a model of reality where God exercises *absolute sway* over the universe (nature, culture, history) in conspicuous isolation and transcendence"[28] (emphasis mine). While it is beyond the scope of this book to go into great detail on these questions, it is important to at least suggest some direction for answers. Philosophers have wrestled with these questions throughout the ages, but the answer will not come from man's wisdom. The pursuit of truth must be guided by the revelation of God.

It is vital to have a firm grip on what we already know about God in Scripture—He is holy, good, righteous, and just. Also it is important to notice that God never robs man of the dignity with which He created him. It is man who has and does rob himself of his dignity.

The Lord Himself says, "I am the LORD, and there is no other. I form the light and create darkness, I bring prosperity and create disaster; I, the LORD, do all these things" (Isaiah 45:6–7). In the following verses He poses a question to those who would protest His workings: "Woe to him who quarrels with his Maker, to him who is but a potsherd . . . Does the clay say to the potter, 'What are you making?'" (Isaiah 45:9).

Does God use evil? It seems that His using anything unholy would be contrary to His nature and His purposes. But we must remember that His ways are not our ways. In Nehemiah 1:8, Nehemiah reminds God of the warning He gave through Moses centuries before: "If you are unfaithful, I will

scatter you." Old Testament history of the nation of Israel
from the time of the judges right through the captivity is re-
plete with examples of God using evil (neighboring pagan
nations) to bring judgment upon His people.

On the matter of God using evil, in his fine work on
providence Paul Helm concludes, "While God ordains moral
evil, he is not the author of it in the sense either that he is
himself morally tainted by what he ordains, or that he takes
away the responsibility of those creatures who perpetrate the
evil."[29] Karl Barth, the great German theologian, concurs as
he says, "The freedom of the human will is not taken away
by God deciding and moving it. He wills to permit its occur-
rence."[30] In the next chapter, we will look at the greatest
example of God ordaining and using evil—the evil that
brought Jesus Christ to the cross.

The image of a tapestry can help us see the big picture in
a different way. As one looks at a tapestry from the back side,
all kinds of threads and colors are visible. Bright yellow,
brown, black, green, orange, and purple twist and turn over
and under each other. There are long threads and short ones
—and even unsightly knots and blotches of color hanging
out. It can appear to be a tangled mess. In our world, it is as
though we are able to see a small part of the tapestry from
the perspective of the back side. We live in the time between
the beginning of the work of art and its glorious completion.
But when the finished tapestry is viewed from the front, it is
a beautiful masterpiece that God has taken pains to shape with
consummate skill. Those knots and loose strings are weaved
into something good. That is how it is with God's work in all
the details in the lives of humanity. That is why we must
walk by faith in Him.[31]

THE FATHER'S HEART

Moses wrote, "He is the Rock, his works are perfect, and all his ways are just. A faithful God who does no wrong, upright and just is he. . . . The eternal God is your refuge, and underneath are the everlasting arms" (Deuteronomy 32:4; 33:27). In a world that is as fallen as ours, hearing that God's ways are perfect is certainly comforting, but God seems to have more to offer us than just an understanding that He holds the world in His hands. We can gather this from verses like Isaiah 40:11 that describe the compassionate love of the Father: "He tends his flock like a shepherd: He gathers the lambs in his arms and carries them close to his heart."

We make note of this before we move to the passion of Jesus Christ because many wonder if God the Father has suffered and knows our pain. We usually hear more about the Son of God having that experience.

The Father entered our world by sending a representative of Himself, His Son, to be Emmanuel, "God with us" (Matthew 1:23). In such condescension, He willingly submitted His Son and His heart to being with His broken people. Through His covenant of love, He opens His divine heart to be hurt, even to the hurts man could inflict on Him, even to the point of death.

In the cross of Christ, the Father "laid on him [the Son] the iniquity of us all" (Isaiah 53:6). This could not take place without the heart of God being deeply moved. When the Son had our sin placed upon Him, the Father turned His head, which is why Jesus cried out, "My God, my God, why have you forsaken me?" (Matthew 27:46).

There is a oneness and intimacy between the Father and the Son (John 10:30), which is beyond our comprehension. Jesus described the ultimate intimate relationship between

Himself and the Father as mutual indwelling (John 17:21–23). In that sense, it could be said that He knows and feels with the Son. Though the human parallel has weaknesses, no loving parents are unmoved when their child suffers.

While most have heard God termed as a Father, His divine caring is actually described in turns of both a mother's and father's love. In Isaiah 49:15–16 God says, "Can a mother forget the baby at her breast and have no compassion on the child she has borne? Though she may forget, I will not forget you! See, I have engraved you on the palms of my hands."

His love is "as high as the heavens are above the earth, so great is his love for those who fear him; as far as the east is from the west, so far has he removed our transgressions from us. As a father has compassion on his children, so the LORD has compassion on those who fear him" (Psalm 103:11–13). So much so, that He sent His Son to pay the penalty that we deserve for our sins. We enter the fellowship of the family of God when we humbly receive the gift of divine grace in the Savior, Jesus Christ. As we shall see, it is in Christ that the Father took the ultimate step to deal with the evil and suffering in our world.

QUESTIONS
FOR REFLECTION

1. Is God secretive about His nature? Explain your conclusion.

2. What is deism? What Scriptures can you cite to rebuke or support this belief?

3. See Jeremiah 18:6 and 2 Corinthians 3:18. How are the concepts in these verses related to suffering you have experienced?

4. The author relates a reminder of God's providence at a difficult time in his family's life. He says, "When one comes to the recognition of God's providence, a decision of faith is necessary." When have you struggled with God's providence?

"All of God's leading is meant to bring people to Himself. His greatest provision toward that end comes in the person of Jesus Christ, who offers the ultimate living picture of God's providence."[32]

■ PROVIDENCE ■

OUT OF THE DARKNESS: HOW JESUS MAKES A DIFFERENCE

THE DELIVERER'S PRICE

IN THE BOOK OF GENESIS, we find a story of providence working in the familiar story of the life of Joseph. Mistreated by his older brothers and sold by them as a slave into Egypt, Joseph suffered through animosity, alienation, isolation, and humiliation. But through it all, God's plan was being developed to save His people from the drought that would strike the region years later.

At the climax of the narrative, the brothers appear before Joseph. They had come to Egypt to buy grain, and found themselves before their brother—gone from the family by their hands years before—who is now in the position of ruler. When they recognized him, they knew that their lives were in his hands, and they expected the worst, because they knew they were guilty of great sin against Joseph. But Joseph's perspective is aligned with God's, and he tells them,

"You intended to harm me, but God intended it for good to accomplish what is now being done, the saving of many lives" (Genesis 50:20).

Redemption came through the suffering of the deliverer.

Just as Joseph's brothers had a deep feeling of guilt and a fearful presumption of retribution because of their past misdeeds, all of us have a sense of future punishment because of our sin. This inbred expectation is part of our innate belief in the "fairness" of the world; we know that we have guilt. The only way this guilt can be removed is through the grace of God and the liberating knowledge of Jesus Christ. He is the ultimate Redeemer.

The apostle Paul said of Jesus Christ, "All things were created by him and for him. He is before all things and in him all things hold together" (Colossians 1:16–17). It is the triune God, the three-in-one of Father, Son, and Holy Spirit, who is the Creator *and* Redeemer of the whole universe. He is both the beginning and the end, and says so Himself: "I am the Alpha and the Omega, the First and the Last, the Beginning and the End" (Revelation 22:13). This chapter will look at Christ and at the Holy Spirit and how these members of the Godhead can make a difference in the life of the sufferer.

GOD'S RESPONSE

God's perfectly calculated and conceived response to fallen humanity is the ultimate expression of divine wisdom. As one could easily imagine, it is in stark contrast to human wisdom. Paul develops this point in 1 Corinthians 1:18–31 when he explains that "God chose the foolish things of the world to shame the wise" (verse 27). He is not saying that we should not seek wisdom; such a notion would be in direct violation of much of Scripture. What he is saying is that God's message sounds like foolishness to those who are perishing (verse 18), and that, therefore, a person who is not yet a believer will not be able to understand eternal matters from God's perspective.

His response was formulated long ago, as the apostle Paul said, "Before the creation of the world" (Ephesians 1:4). It has massive implications for the peril that confronts everyone in this world. God not only deals with evil, but He will, in His time, remove all suffering.

This response in its infinite wisdom and power is really the centerpiece of history—all of God's revelation as well.

What is God's response to fallen humanity?

God's ultimate response to the problem of evil and suffering is the *appearance, death, and resurrection of Christ.*

I am well aware that some reading this may say, "What else is new? I thought you'd say something I haven't heard before." Perhaps I would have joined that chorus at one time as well. Familiarity with the cross of Christ has caused many to minimize its meaning. Discussions about the problem of evil often revolve around trying to let God off the hook. But as the Scottish theologian P. T. Forsyth pointed out in his fine work *The Justification of God,* God really needs no justification. God's response to evil revolves around the justification of man, or redemption. From a biblical perspective, the issue is often pictured in battle terms. God created paradise, and a rebel (Satan) intruded and invaded. Suffering and death were resulting enemies. Mankind is enmeshed in a mortal conflict. It leads us to ask, "Is there any hope that suffering and evil will be overcome?" Yes, in Christ, the greatest enemies of death and evil are defeated. God's answer is evil turned back upon itself, conquered by the ultimate degree of love in the fulfillment of justice.[33]

The death and resurrection of Jesus Christ is the anchor

of God's design for redemption and the reversal of all suffering. The cross was no accident. Christ was handed over to be crucified by wicked men "by God's set purpose and foreknowledge. . . . But God raised him from the dead, freeing him from the agony of death" (Acts 2:23–24). Still, the question remains valid—Why did God choose to defeat evil *this* way?

MOTIVATION AND MECHANICS

Any consideration of God's response to our suffering must first recognize that the motivation for His response is His infinite love. Because of love He got personally involved at great personal cost. He went through the world's greatest suffering, as a participant. This sets Him apart from any other deity.

In the immortal words of the Bible: "For God so loved the world that he gave his one and only Son, that whoever believes in him shall not perish but have eternal life" (John 3:16). Fueled by His limitless power and guided by His perfect wisdom, this divine love sent His own perfect Son to an imperfect world.

God first had to deal with the cause of suffering—sin. Secondly, He dealt with death in all of its forms and power. To deal with the *guilt* of sin, there must be a *turnaround* and *payment* of the penalty. To deal with the *broken relationship* caused by sin, there must be *reconciliation*. This process would require Him to personally come down to earth and to take into Himself the ultimate suffering so that it could be removed.

Because Jesus was fully human as well as fully divine, He went through the gamut of human experiences and emotions, just as we do. He must have had much joy in His time on earth—He socialized, He taught multitudes, and we can certainly infer that He found much joy in healing, in freeing many from demonic oppression, and in restoring to life loved ones who had died (see Matthew 9:18–26; Luke 7:11–15; John 11:40–44).

And yet, as the one who is the beginning and the end of all things, Christ certainly understood the tribulations that are part of life on this earth. He Himself also knew and experienced sorrow and suffering. As the prophet of old accurately described Him, He was "despised and rejected by men, a man of sorrows and familiar with suffering" (Isaiah 53:3; also see Hebrews 5:7–9). It was here, away from the glories of heaven, that He experienced life as man in a corrupt world.

Leading up to the cross, Jesus suffered what might be identified as anticipatory suffering. He knew full well the pain He would endure and informed His disciples of the agony He would experience (Matthew 16:21). Some of our greatest suffering comes as we anticipate the reality of suffering or death. In the garden where He was praying before His arrest, He told His disciples He was "overwhelmed with sorrow to the point of death" (Matthew 26:38). As He spoke to those who came to arrest Him, He uttered some poignant words describing these hours as the time "when darkness reigns" (Luke 22:53). The crucifixion would be the ultimate suffering of all history. This apex would also become the "breaking point" of suffering.

While most popular depictions of the death of Christ are mainly focused on the physical pain of it, Christ's greatest suffering on the cross was spiritual. The sound of these anguish-filled words haunts all history: "My God, my God, why have you forsaken me?" (Matthew 27:46). He felt a separation from God greater than that of the worst criminal. Upon Him was placed the sin of the world and with it came the wrath and judgment of the holy God (2 Corinthians 5:21) as foretold in Isaiah 53:6. This was the only way to deal with sin in righteousness and justice. The penalty was to take the *curse* of sin upon Himself (Galatians 3:13). He felt the pains of hell with all their pain, weight, and pressure. This was the most horrible and awful suffering. The heavenly Father could not look on the sin and had to condemn it. As Pascal wrote, "This punishment is inflicted by no human, but an almighty hand, and only he that is almighty can bear it."[34] Jesus now knew the utter isolation of being abandoned by all.

But He was not defeated. Jesus had a deep awareness of His suffering *and* its purpose: "Now my heart is troubled, and what shall I say? 'Father, save me from this hour'? No, it was for this very reason I came to this hour. Father, glorify your name!" (John 12:27–28). This suffering and death did not surprise Him. When He said, "It is finished!" He knew that He had accomplished His mission.

Though the Father turned His face temporarily from the Son, He would not leave Him in death. The Son had within Him "the power of an indestructible life" (Hebrews 7:16). Some of the most exciting words in the Bible were Peter's when he wrote, "God raised him from the dead, freeing him from the agony of death, because it was impossible for death to keep its hold on him" (Acts 2:24). Through the resurrection, the death knell for death itself was sounded loud and clear. Through the victory of the Savior, eternal salvation for us was born.

STRENGTH FOR TODAY

Jesus made it possible for a restored and reconciled relationship with God. "For Christ died for sins once for all, the righteous for the unrighteous, to bring you to God" (1 Peter

3:18). Through the *death* of Christ came the way for eternal *life* for anyone who believes in Jesus Christ as his Savior (Colossians 3:4).

Not only is the cross of Christ the divine response to evil and suffering, but it is the unfolding of the great heart of God. When we pass through the valley of suffering, He is not only with us, but He understands and is able to sympathize: "For we do not have a high priest who is unable to sympathize with our weaknesses, but we have one who has been tempted in every way, just as we are" (Hebrews 4:15; also see Isaiah 53:3 and 1 Peter 5:7).

The mystery of the Father's will that He purposed in Christ is *still* being put into effect. Now He is portrayed to be at the Father's right hand where "he must reign until he has put all his enemies under his feet. The last enemy to be destroyed is death" (1 Corinthians 15:25–26). The Scriptures teach that He will come back to earth and remove all evil, pain, and suffering. Then it will be true that "death has been swallowed up in victory" (1 Corinthians 15:54). "All things in heaven and on earth [will be brought] together under one head, even Christ" (Ephesians 1:10).

As the prophecy of Scripture indicates, there will be a day when "the dwelling of God is with men . . . He will wipe every tear from their eyes. There will be no more death or mourning or crying or pain" (Revelation 21:3–4). In this sense, the greatest is yet to come when He makes everything new. Even creation itself is eager for the day when paradise will be regained:

> For all creation is waiting eagerly for that future day when God will reveal who his children really are. Against its will, everything on earth was subjected to God's curse. All creation anticipates the day when it will join God's children in

glorious freedom from death and decay. For we know that all creation has been groaning as in the pains of childbirth right up to the present time. And even we Christians, although we have the Holy Spirit within us as a foretaste of future glory, also groan to be released from pain and suffering. We, too, wait anxiously for that day when God will give us our full rights as his children, including the new bodies he has promised us.

—Romans 8:19–23 NLT

The reality of the future and final working of God becomes the cornerstone of a theology of hope. Because of the past and present working of God, the one who knows Him through Jesus Christ has a "living hope" (1 Peter 1:3). That hope becomes a beam of light in the darkest night, and it fills the believer with anticipation as they are on their journey (Titus 2:11–14). The power of this hope ("the glorious appearing of Jesus Christ") cannot be measured. Though there is physical suffering and loss, this hope burns bright within. In my darkness, this hope has been a beacon, like that of the lighthouse, which has shined brighter and brighter. As the response of God to suffering has Christ as the centerpiece, so our response must have Christ at the center as our Light. To miss Him is to remain in darkness on many levels.

At the heart of the issue is faith, which causes one to be transformed from death to life, darkness to light (Acts 26:18; Colossians 1:13). As Jesus of Nazareth said, "Whoever hears my word and *believes* him who sent me has eternal life . . . he has crossed over from death to life" (John 5:24, emphasis mine). Without the response of faith in the working of God in Christ, a turning to Him, there can be no light or life—either now or in the future. This new life as revealed in the Word of God begins in the here and now. It is the source of all truly successful navigation of the unmapped darkness. I would not assume that all who are reading these words have taken that initial step of faith in Christ as Lord and Savior. If you have not, let me invite you to do so today.

Others of you may think, "I'm already familiar with all this." Fair enough. But let me say that it is absolutely necessary to revisit the foundation especially in the time of affliction. When we're dealing with the monumentally difficult issues of tackling evil and suffering, we must get back to the big picture, to put an eternal perspective on these things. It is at the foundation that we gain strength to not only withstand the storm but to be as the apostle Paul said, "More than conquerors through him who loved us." Indeed, nothing "will be able to separate us from the love of God that is in Christ Jesus our Lord" (Romans 8:37–39). This victorious note seems lacking from much of Christianity. I have needed this assurance in times of great trial, and still do, immensely. It was and is only through focusing on the foundations of faith that victory and joy come. Christ came to "bind up the brokenhearted . . . and release from darkness for the prisoners . . . to comfort all who mourn . . . to bestow on them a crown of beauty instead of ashes, the oil of gladness instead of mourning, and a garment of praise instead of a spirit of despair. They will be called oaks of righteousness" (Isaiah 61:1–3). And He has done all this and more through His resurrection power. Having gained this understanding, it is possible to move on to more answers and healing.

THE GREAT SHEPHERD

In examining the foundation of the universe, and reviewing God's response to the fall of His creation by offering His only Son as atonement for the sin that resulted in the fall, we next will discuss one role of Jesus, that is, of God as our shepherd.

Perhaps the greatest analogy of the providence of God in Christ is revealed in the shepherd metaphor, with many Old and New Testament references to it (Psalms 28:9; 80:1; Ecclesiastes 12:11; Isaiah 40:11; Ezekiel 34; Hebrews 13:20; 1 Peter 2:25; 5:4). Painting a portrait of His role as Guide and Savior of people of all nations, Jesus said of Himself:

> "I am the good shepherd; I know my sheep and my sheep know me—just as the Father knows me and I know the Father—and I lay down my life for the sheep. I have other sheep that are not of this sheep pen. I must bring them also. They too will listen to my voice, and there shall be one flock and one shepherd. The reason my Father loves me is that I lay down my life—only to take it up again. No one takes it from me, but I lay it down of my own accord. I have authority to lay it down and authority to take it up again. This command I received from my Father."
>
> —John 10:14–18

In the well-known Twenty-third Psalm, David begins by declaring his dependence on the Lord: "The LORD is my shepherd." This is where you and I need to start as well. When we experience suffering and trouble, it is not explanations and logic that we need. It is the knowledge of the presence of the Shepherd—*then* we will be able to hear His voice and follow Him. As He leads us, we can say with David, "Even though I walk through the valley of the shadow of death, I will fear no evil, for you are with me" (Psalm 23:4).

The focus must be turned back to the Shepherd. This is a choice—a vital choice for anyone passing through adversity. The person traveling through deep darkness is content when he knows the heavenly Guide is present and leading him through it all. To glance at the perilous surroundings is only natural. But in the meantime, we get to know Him better as we continue with Him day by day, as well as throughout all eternity. In a beautiful glimpse of heaven in Revelation 7:17, we read: "For the Lamb at the center of the throne will be their shepherd; he will lead them to springs of living water. And God will wipe away every tear from their eyes."

Through the Holy Spirit

We know the Father and the Son, but we must never discount the role of the Holy Spirit in our lives, whether in the daily concerns of life or at times of trial and suffering.

Some of the greatest words of Christ were spoken just before His passion as He prepared the disciples for His departure and the suffering they would face. He promised them the greatest gift—the Holy Spirit who would come and dwell in them (John 14:15–26; Acts 1:4; 1 Corinthians 6:19).

The presence and work of the Holy Spirit is what "keeps the believer together." Without His help, it is nearly impossible to avoid despair and fight against the lies of the world and the Evil One. When Jesus promised in John 16:13 to send the Spirit, He said the Spirit would guide "into all truth":

No one knows the thoughts of God except the Spirit of God. We have not received the spirit of the world but the Spirit who is from God, that we may understand what God has freely given us. This is what we speak, not in words taught us by human wisdom but in words taught by the Spirit, expressing spiritual truths in spiritual words. The man without the Spirit does not accept the things that come from the Spirit of God, for they are foolishness to him, and he cannot understand them, because they are spiritually discerned. The spiritual man makes judgments about all things, but he himself is not subject to any man's judgment: "For who has known the mind of the Lord that he may instruct him?" But we have the mind of Christ.

—1 Corinthians 2:11–16

He has ignited an eternal flame of hope, for which He only could be viewed as the fuel that makes that hope brighter and brighter—even in the darkness. He is the Illuminator opening the eyes of our hearts to see the glory and light of Christ. "I keep asking that the God of our Lord Jesus Christ, the glorious Father, may give you the Spirit of wisdom and revelation, so that you may know him better. I pray also that the eyes of your heart may be enlightened" (Ephesians 1:17–18). We know that He lives in us when we are being guided by the Word of God (Psalms 119:92; 105; 130). Many times He has spoken strengthening comfort to me through the Psalms. We know He is in us because Jesus promised Him. John 14:16–21 is a classic passage of the promise of the Spirit. His indwelling of the believer is confirmed in 1 Corinthians 6:19. He will direct us to what our hearts need, but we must surrender to "be filled with the Spirit" (Ephesians 5:18) and to not stifle His leading (1 Thessalonians 5:19).

The Spirit doesn't use a megaphone, but His ministry is more like the "gentle whisper" similar to that which Elijah the prophet experienced (1 Kings 19:12). He speaks especially in the quiet of a heart simply trusting in the Lord (Psalms 42:5–8; 46:10; 62:1–2, 5–8; Isaiah 30:15). If we listen, He will reassure us of the Father's loving arms around us:

For you did not receive a spirit that makes you a slave again to fear, but you received the Spirit of sonship. And by him we cry, "Abba, Father." The Spirit himself testifies with our spirit that we are God's children. Now if we are children, then we are heirs—heirs of God and co-heirs with Christ, if indeed we share in his sufferings in order that we may also share in his glory.

—Romans 8:15–17

He is at work in us to conform us to the image of Christ. As film must be developed in the darkroom, some of God's transforming work must be done "in the darkness." It is the divine process to produce a beautiful life. Just on a personal note, I know that I'm more tender to the hardships and tragedies of others who have lost dear ones, as my wife and I lost our newborn son, and as I was later to lose my wife.

Finally, the empowering leading of the Spirit is vital if we're to find the lighted path and take the steps that seem beyond our strength (Ephesians 3:16–19). Through the power of the Holy Spirit the Christian pilgrim will move through the darkness into light one step at a time.

> Holy Spirit, faithful Guide
> ever at the Christian's side
> ever present truest Friend,
> ever near Thine aid to lend.
> Leaves us not to doubt and fear,
> groping on in darkness drear;
> when the storms are raging sore,
> hearts grow faint, and hopes give o'er.
> Whisper softly, "Wand'rer, come!
> Follow Me. I'll guide thee home."[35]

QUESTIONS
FOR REFLECTION

1. *Do you agree with the author's statement that it is "absolutely necessary to revisit the foundation, especially in the
time of affliction"?*

2. *According to the author, what is God's ultimate response to
suffering? How is this response the "centerpiece of history"?
How is the crucifixion both the "ultimate suffering of all history" and the "breaking point of suffering"?*

3. *What is the "victorious note (that) seems to be lacking from
much of Christianity"? Do you agree? Explain why or why
not.*

4. *When it comes to the message of the cross, do you ever feel as
if you've heard it all before? The author says that "familiarity
with the cross has caused many to minimize its meaning."
Do you agree? Recall how you decided to believe Jesus'
claims about who He is and live your life for Him. What
brought you to this decision? How does this memory give
freshness to the message? If you have not made this decision,
think through what you believe about Christ and what questions you might still have about Him.*

"Dear friends, do not be surprised at the painful trial you are suffering, as though something strange were happening to you. But rejoice that you participate in the sufferings of Christ, so that you may be overjoyed when his glory is revealed."

■ 1 Peter 4:12–13 ■

RIDING IT OUT: THE VALUE OF SUFFERING

JUST THREE MONTHS AFTER my wife passed away, I found myself in the hospital again. This time, it was my three sons who were in the waiting room, and it was I who was lying in a hospital bed, post–heart attack. There I was, tubes coming out of me and questioning God all over again. My sons had come close to not only losing their mother, but now their father. I was glad that wasn't the case and that I was alive, but there seemed to be no reason for the kind of suffering our family had been through in such a short time.

The boys were twenty-one, seventeen, and twelve then —young to lose their mother.

The reality of being a single parent was still with me when I got home. There was cooking, laundry, bills, a career transition, the boys' needs, my prescribed recuperation— and all these responsibilities were mine. I couldn't help but cry when I would think of the impossibility of being both mother and father to my sons.

What good could come of this?

DEBUNKING INSTANT GRATIFICATION

We live in a culture that worships pleasure. Our pay-checks, leisure time, and dreams are devoted to it. Anything that denies us happiness is termed *hard, painful,* or even *evil.* We overestimate both the goodness of pleasure *and* the bad-ness of pain. A material blessing is coveted and won, only to lose its appeal once familiar. A delay in our plans or the snub of another deprive us of pleasure, and even these minor oc-currences can throw our moods south.

Modern man is deceived by the vice known as short-term thinking.[36] A focus on the here and now blinds us to more important matters. We are prone to neglect a better, albeit a challenging, way of life in order to grab hold of that which is only decent but easily obtained.

This is the way of the child. If a little boy receives five dollars a week in allowance, he will likely empty the ice cream truck shortly after hearing its siren song, instead of saving for the future. If he saved his five dollars, he could purchase a new bicycle by the time he is capable of riding alone.

In a more serious example, a husband and wife may choose to work overtime to obtain the "good life" and be happy. If they are not careful, they may neglect their rela-tionship and soon wonder why their marriage is suffering af-ter gaining many of the material pleasures they have always wanted.

We do not respond easily to our best-laid plans going awry.

Often when we suffer, our focus is altered beyond the immediate situation. Some people—perhaps for the first time—consider important, eternal matters, possibly the claims of the gospel itself. Trying to bear the pain and sorrow of this fallen world without God's help will not lead a person to deep healing. In contrast, asking God for His help in letting this time of suffering not be wasted can lead to a richer relationship with Him.

It is natural for us as human beings to seek understanding of the world around us, especially as it relates to our own lives. But we do not need to understand everything; we cannot in this life.

At the memorial service in Washington, D.C., following the tragedy of September 11, 2001, Billy Graham's remarks included the following:

> "But how do we understand something like this? [the 9/11 attacks]. Why does God allow evil like this to take place? Perhaps that is what you are asking now. You may even be angry at God. I want to assure you that God understands these feelings that you may have. We've seen so much on our television, heard on our radio, stories that bring tears to our eyes and make us all feel a sense of anger. But God can be trusted, even when life seems at its darkest.

> "But what are some of the lessons we can learn? First, we are reminded of the mystery and reality of evil. I've been asked hundreds of times in my life why God allows tragedy and suffering. I have to confess that I really do not know the answer totally, even to my own satisfaction. I have to accept by faith that God is sovereign, and He's a God of love and mercy and compassion in the midst of suffering."[37]

When we experience suffering in our lives, it is foolish to reject God or become embittered. But whether or not we're going through suffering of some kind or another, it is always best to maintain our relationship with the Creator, and then continue to seek a deeper understanding of His purpose for us.

Martha and Mary, not to mention the entire town of Bethany, learned this lesson following the death of Lazarus. Jesus did nothing while His friend Lazarus was sick, intentionally waiting for him to die (John 11:6). After he died, many were saddened; even Jesus wept (verse 35), proving that as a human He felt the sting of the death of a friend. Some were embittered, questioning Jesus and doubting His providence. But the purpose of God became clear when Jesus told Lazarus to come out of the tomb. Some believe the only purpose of this miracle was to display the power of the Son of God. This *was* demonstrated, but the narrative shows us that in addition, the expansion of the kingdom was part of the plan since many put their faith in Christ that day (John 12:9–11).

For these reasons, in any and all circumstances—good ones as well as bad—it is always wise to reflect upon what purposes for the kingdom of God the circumstances might be producing. Suffering and pain may become blessings in disguise. God intrudes in our lives through the door of affliction. As C. S. Lewis wrote, "God whispers to us in our pleasures, speaks in our conscience, but shouts in our pains: It is his megaphone to rouse a deaf world."[38] Because it is so easy for us to not listen to His more gentle calls, we can pray, "Lord, help us to see You, know You, and hear Your voice at this time."

THE PURPOSE OF GLORY

If we understand and believe that the Lord has some answers for us, we will go to Him. If we do not believe, we will go elsewhere for answers, or we may resign ourselves to ignorance. Because of who God reveals Himself to be in the Bible, we know of some specific ways God uses suffering.

Some of God's works are preparatory or "seed works," while others bring His designs to completion. It is like a kaleidoscope, fitted with various pieces and colors. Designs and images begin to take shape as the view is shifted and adjusted by turning the apparatus. In the same way, the pieces and parts of our lives and stories begin to take shape as we are given a glimpse of (1) how God sees our struggles, and (2) how "all things work for the good of those who love him, who have been called according to his purpose" (Romans 8:28).

There is one ultimate purpose that is above all others and to which all others contribute in some way, and that is the glory of God. As the psalmist declared, *glory* is the reason behind creation in the first place: "The heavens declare the glory of God" (Psalm 19:1).

The glorification of God is best exemplified in the life and death of Jesus Christ. Jesus said to the Father, "I have brought you glory on earth by completing the work you gave me to do" (John 17:4). As Jesus faced the ultimate suffering on the cross, He expressed His troubled heart. He also voiced His heart's desire, "Father, glorify your name" (John 12:28). This was the paramount desire of Christ, and it can be in our lives, too, even amidst painful suffering. Seeking to be a participant in the glory of Christ is what gave Holocast survivor Corrie ten Boom hope even in concentration camps. Corrie writes:

> I had been sustaining myself from my Scriptures a verse at a time; now like a starving man I gulped entire Gospels at a reading, seeing whole the magnificent drama of salvation.
>
> And as I did, an incredible thought prickled the back of my neck. Was it possible that this—all of this that seemed so

wasteful and so needless—this war, Scheveningen prison, this
very cell, none of it was unforeseen or accidental? Could it be
part of the pattern first revealed in the Gospels? Hadn't Jesus
—and here my reading became intent indeed—hadn't Jesus
been defeated as utterly and unarguably as our little group
and our small plans had been?

But if the Gospels were truly the pattern of God's activity,
then defeat was only the beginning. I would look around at
the bare little cell and wonder what conceivable victory could
come from a place like this. . . .

Life in Ravensbruck took place on two separate levels,
mutually impossible. One, the observable, external life, grew
every day more horrible. The other, the life we lived with
God, grew daily better, truth upon truth, glory upon glory.[39]

As one moves through the darkness, it is good to ask:
"How can this experience be used for the glory of God?" In
this way, we become aligned with the greatest purpose of all.

Union with Christ

Suffering most greatly affects our spiritual person, the
inner man. Through suffering, God intends that our focus
on Christ be ever sharper and constant. The only thing that
really helps put suffering in perspective is Christ—His cross,
resurrection, and present glorification in heaven. Once a
person accepts Christ as Savior, he is united to Christ in a
supernatural way (Romans 6:3–8). In the darkness of suffering, the truth that "Christ in you [is] the hope of glory" becomes deeply significant as the believer longs for Christ to
work in and though him (Colossians 1:27).

Surrender to Christ does pose a challenge: death to self.
Jesus Himself spoke of this in His call to discipleship, "If

anyone would come after me, he must deny himself and take up his cross daily and follow me" (Luke 9:23). Whoever serves Him must follow Him in the way of suffering. In contemplating the cross of Christ, we see One who willingly gave Himself completely to do the will of the Father (see Philippians 2:8–11).

In his classic work *City of God,* Augustine describes a key difference between God's kingdom and this world's focus on the exaltation of self: "Humility is highly prized in the City of God . . . and it receives particular emphasis in the character of Christ, the king of that City."[40]

There is a sense of loss as we loosen our grip on our ambitions, desires, and creature comforts. God may allow some of these to remain, while some plans will be shattered. Peter Kreeft describes death to self as "the essence of both suffering and joy."[41] We, too, can embrace Paul's wisdom that said, "I consider everything a loss compared to the surpassing greatness of knowing Christ Jesus my Lord, for whose sake I have lost all things" (Philippians 3:8).

One of the major keys to dying to self is embracing what Paul described when he said, "I have been crucified with Christ and I no longer live, but Christ lives in me" (Galatians 2:20). We are called to no longer conform to the pattern of thinking that belongs to the world, but to "be transformed by the renewing of your mind" (Romans 12:2). His control is needed since ego and pride war against the Christian's new nature for control of the will, and we cannot put to death the sinful nature on our own. Through the power of Christ's death and resurrection, we die to it and "rise up" as new creations with the Holy Spirit as our guide (see Romans 8:1–17; 2 Corinthians 5:17–18). As the cross brought suffering, then joy—we find this is often the case as we continually surrender ourselves to Christ. We must not forget the *joy* part either,

for it is central to the character of God. In *The Weight of Glory,*
C. S. Lewis reminds us that His desires are perfect:

> We are told to deny ourselves and take up our crosses in order
> that we may follow Christ; and nearly every description of
> what we shall ultimately find if we do so contains an appeal to
> desire. If there lurks in most modern minds the notion that to
> desire our own good and earnestly to hope for the enjoyment
> of it is a bad thing, I submit that this notion has crept in from
> Kant and the Stoics and is no part of the Christian faith. In-
> deed, if we consider the unblushing promises of reward and
> the staggering nature of rewards promised in the Gospels, it
> would seem that Our Lord finds our desires not too strong,
> but too weak. We are half-hearted creatures, fooling about
> with drink and sex and ambition when infinite joy is offered
> us, like an ignorant child who wants to go on making mud pies
> in a slum because he cannot imagine what is meant by the
> offer of a holiday at the sea.[42]

GRACE AND POWER

Living in this fallen world causes us to become painfully
aware of our weaknesses. Suffering only intensifies this
awareness, but it also becomes the avenue through which
one can know the great power of God. Who hasn't thought,
"I can't do this! It is too much for me to bear. It's impossible!" As we see our total insufficiency without God, His
grace becomes our sufficiency (2 Corinthians 1:9; 3:5).
Grace is the spiritual empowerment or enablement that God
gives us in our time of need. In answer to Paul's prayer for
the removal of suffering, the Lord said *no.* What He did say
was, "My grace is sufficient for you, for my power is made
perfect in weakness," to which Paul responded, "Therefore I

will boast all the more gladly about my weaknesses, so that Christ's power may rest on me . . . I delight in weaknesses, in insults, in hardships, in persecutions, in difficulties. For when I am weak, then I am strong" (2 Corinthians 12:9–10). It is an amazing thing, then, that suffering becomes a servant of God. "Weakness is the paradoxical mode of the power of Christ."[43] In this sense suffering is desecrated, dethroned, and becomes a slave to joy and the power of God is displayed in its glory (Romans 5:3; James 1:2–4).

This sounds totally ridiculous to the person who does not know God and His heart. To the mind outside of Christ's indwelling, suffering is an omen of the ultimate enemy— death. The eyes of flesh see only fright, but the eyes of faith see the etchings of the fingers of God. Since the power of God brings victory, suffering is an occasion to know the power of God at work in us. This is expressed positively in the immortal words, "I can do everything through him [Christ] who gives me strength" (Philippians 4:13). To have that kind of strength in a fallen world takes faith and persistence to seek daily renewal through the Holy Spirit and the Word of God.

As the writer of Hebrews put it, there is the temptation "to throw away your confidence" (Hebrews 10:35). In this process, it is important to recognize that God is still doing a work. This reality was expressed well by Joni Eareckson Tada, who was paralyzed at the age of seventeen in a swimming accident. She compares God's gracious nurturing and restoration of her life to the clearing of a garden:

> It is no longer a mystery now that I've felt the crunch of
> decades of paralysis. The encroachments of my limitations
> often feel like the cutting edge of a spade, digging up twisted
> vines of self-centeredness and the dirt of sin and rebellion.

Uprooting rights. Clearing out the debris of habitual sins. Shoveling away pride. To believe in God in the midst of suffering is to empty myself; and to empty myself is to increase the capacity—the pond area—for God. The greatest good suffering can do for me is to increase my capacity for God. Then he, like a spring, is free to flow through me.[44]

It is comforting for us to remember, however, that Joni did not arrive at this point in her faithfulness easily. The story of her struggles is told in her books. Her journey of faithfulness is all the more victorious because of its difficulty.

REFINED BY FIRE

"I am going to do something in your days." Those words of God to a prophet (Habakkuk 1:5) are still true in our times. Just as God is at work, what He is looking for today is what He's always desired. What is He seeking? Second Chronicles 16:9 tells us His "eyes . . . range throughout the earth to strengthen those whose hearts are fully committed to him." Regardless of the circumstances of those His eyes see, He is looking for a living, active, and obedient faith.

To be sure, this faith, this resolve to trust Him come what may, will be tested! In this respect, nothing has changed since the beginning. All the patriarchs from Adam through the prophets were rewarded for their faithful adherence to God amidst the trials they faced. Although Noah had never seen an ocean and could have spent his time in recreational pleasure instead of toiling to build a boat, he followed God's blueprint. Although Abraham loathed the thought of walking up the mountain with his son, knife in hand, he followed God's instructions. Although Joseph could have exacted revenge on his brothers, he followed God's directive. Although Jeremiah would not have chosen a cistern as his abode or gall as his food, he followed God's calling and command. As an example to us, those who lived and acted by faith are named in a sort of divine "hall of faith" found in Hebrews 11. In the chapter that follows, we are pointed to the greatest model, Christ, who "endured the cross, scorning its shame, and sat down at the right hand of the throne of God. Consider him who endured such opposition from sinful men, so that you will not grow weary and lose heart" (Hebrews 12:2–3).

Through testing, we come to see if our faith is genuine (1 Peter 1:6–7). It is not that God needs to figure out if our faith is real, for He already knows. But when we are refined, we see where our loyalties and priorities lie and, therefore, are spurred on in our pursuit, trust, and service of God.

When our faith becomes stronger, its impurities having been burnt away, we are all the more blessed since we are closer to God in His holiness. Our faith is challenged, refined, and strengthened when our desires are in conflict with God's will, and yet we still choose to follow Him. As the psalmist pointed out, "For you, O God, tested us; you refined us like silver. . . . We went through fire and water, but you brought us to a place of abundance" (Psalm 66:8–12).

We are exhorted to persevere, stand fast, and rejoice: "Do not throw away your confidence; it will be richly rewarded. You need to persevere so that when you have done the will of God, you will receive what he has promised" (Hebrews 10:35–36).

God will help. He invites us to call on Him to be "strengthened with all power according to his glorious might so that you may have great endurance and patience . . ." (Colossians 1:11). The test, then, becomes an opportunity to know and embrace the power of God. Patient, humble endurance is the mark of living in harmony with Christ who endured all things for us. Suffering shapes us into tools that are more fit for the Master's use (2 Timothy 2:21). Each servant of Christ, every believer, must make choices each time as to how he or she will respond when placed on the divine anvil. It is a choice between faith, fellowship, and fruitfulness—or fear, frustration, isolation, and failure. But this choice is a process that is not so easily done; the Christian must go through this process and make these choices repeatedly. But God has promised to be with us and grant us the knowledge of Himself, His power, and His great love.

The following words of Julian of Norwich have been of great encouragement to me: "In return for the little pain we suffer here on earth, we shall have an exalted, endless knowledge of God, which we could never have without that."[45]

IN HIS IMAGE

What is the ultimate purpose for the Christian, after all? Paul says, "We proclaim him, admonishing and teaching everyone with all wisdom, so that we may present everyone perfect in Christ" (Colossians 1:28; also see 3:10). The ultimate purpose for the Christian, then, is that there be a transformation into the image of Christ.

We are encouraged to put off disobedience and any hindrance to growth. This often happens through God's correction in our lives. In many of the Psalms, David referred to God's discipline as the pathway to confession and repentance (see Psalms 32:2–5 and 51). This working of God may be due to our wrongdoing, though this is certainly not always so, as in the case of Job.

In Hebrews, God's discipline is compared to that of a Father:

We have all had human fathers who disciplined us and we re-
spected them for it. How much more should we submit to the
Father of our spirits and live! Our fathers disciplined us for a
little while as they thought best; but God disciplines us for our
good, that we may share in his holiness. No discipline seems
pleasant at the time, but painful. Later on, however, it pro-
duces a harvest of righteousness and peace for those who have
been trained by it.

—Hebrews 12:9–11

If one is resisting submission to God, he will not receive
instruction concerning the suffering brought into his life. On
the other hand, His wise child will be ready to learn, and
through understanding he will be drawn closer to the Lord.

God uses suffering as education to teach us vital lessons
and transform us. In this process, He transforms our person
and He also changes our perspectives on life. We begin to realize what is really important in life. Our priorities, values,
and affections are directly impacted (Colossians 3:1–4). Suffering has a way of humbling us and changing our views of
people and relationships. We realize our oneness with all of
suffering humanity. As a result, we can begin to see people
through the eyes of Christ and relate to them in love as He
does. And if we never suffer, we have little comfort to offer
to others. "Praise be to the God . . . who comforts us in all
our troubles, so that we can comfort those in any trouble
with the comfort we ourselves have received from God"
(2 Corinthians 1:3–4).

As suffering accomplishes its work, one begins to realize
the benefits. It was expressed well in the words, "Before I
was afflicted [humbled] I went astray, but now I obey your
word. It was good for me to be afflicted so that I might learn
your decrees" (Psalm 119:67, 71). For a perfect example of

submission to the Father's will, we must turn again to Christ. With cries and tears He prayed to the Father, and "although he was a son, he learned obedience from what he suffered" (Hebrews 5:8). The problem often is that we are slow learners. As I have passed through various times of trouble, it has become apparent that we need to ask the question, *Lord, what are You trying to teach me through this?* The major issue is learning obedience—submission of our will to His will.

Take an everyday example. A team of aspiring young soccer players chase the ball around in a blur of mindless confusion. It is a tangled mass of energy and desire, with each and every player following the other and the ball in a continuously changing puzzle. Although they have desire to succeed, the players' efforts result in complete disaster. The only solution is a coach who tells players what to do and when to do it. He forces them to do what they do not want to do: stay in position and stop chasing the ball. Until their collective will is made subordinate to the will of the coach, all their efforts will be in vain. But when they follow his teaching, they can succeed.

In the same way, as individuals in God's family, we must submit our will to God's will. The team of the church is only effective when we operate in harmony and under the direction of the Omniscient One.

EXPECTING VICTORY

Living completely in union with Christ brings an inner freedom unknown to most. As the Christian remains in— lives in—abides in—Christ, he can live in the victory of Christ (John 15:1–5). Through faith in Christ, one is freed from the penalty and power of sin as pointed out in Romans chapters 5–8. While we still struggle with sin and sometimes experience physical pain and affliction, in Christ we are freed from spiritual suffering and death.

When we realize that He carried away our guilt, we are liberated from the bondage to all sin and suffering and are given a matchless freedom (John 8:32, 36). The contemplation of Christ's death and resurrection brings this deep inner awareness of our liberation. In the future, the physical liberation will be experienced in the final and complete accomplishment of our salvation—we will receive new bodies for our eternal life in heaven (see 1 Corinthians 15:35–57).

Meanwhile, we can participate in the victory and realize the power of the life of Christ in the present. We have new and eternal life flowing through our veins (John 7:38–39; 2 Corinthians 5:17). Jesus said, "In me you may have peace. In this world you will have trouble [suffering]. But take heart! I have overcome the world" (John 16:33).

Keeping our focus on the end goal helps us endure suffering. God is training and encouraging us so that we "run with perseverance the race marked out for us" (Hebrews 12:1). Winning the prize of fulfilling Christ's purposes for us involves "forgetting what is behind and straining toward what is ahead" (Philippians 3:13).

If we focus on the pain and lose hope, we can easily fall into despair and futility. Many of the soldiers who died in the Japanese prison camps of World War II lost hope prior to succumbing to death. Conversely, many of those who survived disease, abuse, forced labor, and torture possessed a belief that their hope for liberation was not in vain. Their hope helped keep them alive.

The people in our times have been so weighed down by life in this fallen world that it is only natural that a culture of despair has developed. Suffering surfaces what kind of hope lives in the heart of a person. For the most part, people have fixed their hope on things in this world. "If only for this life we have hope in Christ, we are to be pitied more than all men" (1 Corinthians 15:19). We *do* have hope in this life—but that's not all. Knowing Christ and growing in intimacy with Him is a journey that leads up to something eternally bigger and better.

As Christians we should have expectations. Just as Christ *"for the joy set before him* endured the cross" (Hebrews 12:2, emphasis mine) in anticipation of His second coming and being rightfully exalted, so we "wait for the blessed hope—the glorious appearing of our great God and Savior, Jesus Christ" (Titus 2:13). He will be faithful to His promise: "I will come back and take you to be with me" (John 14:3).

The route to heaven is not easy, and may even be a grind, but the arrival at the destination is worth it. For example, suppose a family from Chicago decides to take a vacation to the beach in Florida during spring break. The children go along for free, of course, and they have no responsibilities to help drive the car. In March, the weather in the Windy City can be fickle. It may be sleeting one day and mild the next. Florida's beaches beckon with a youthful delight.

So imagine the shock if one of the children informs the parents that he doesn't want to take the trip because he doesn't like riding in the car while it is sleeting. Or imagine if he refuses to go because he doesn't like driving through mountains. Or he doesn't like eating out. Or he doesn't want to be in the car for twenty hours. Or he doesn't want to have to use a public restroom.

The child bears absolutely no responsibility for the cost or arrangements of the trip. All of it has been paid for and he is fully entitled to enjoy himself at the beach for a week. Surely he would endure these minor difficulties to participate in a week of pure joy.

How much more should the Christian endure the traveling troubles on this earth to arrive at our perfect eternal destination? There is no necessity to make the sad return trip back to a fallen world. There is no cost—Christ has paid it all.

Jesus Christ endured the greatest tribulations so that our reservation at our destination (heaven) is secured. He is the greatest example of faithful, patient perseverance. He endured the cross, the insults of sinful men, and intense sufferings of every type to provide an eternal salvation (Hebrews 2:2–3).

Hope in Christ stands in stark contrast to the paralysis or passiveness that would rather lie down and die. Because Christ is victorious over sin and death, that victory is ours as believers—ultimately and in day-to-day living. The apostle said, "We are more than conquerors through him who loved us" (Romans 8:37). But it is up to us whether we will live in the victory of Christ or instead harden our hearts.

JUSTICE DONE

There is another side to suffering. We already know that sin brought judgment and suffering for the race (Genesis 3; Romans 1:18 ff.; 5:12–18). Sometimes, suffering is actually the here-and-now judgment of God upon man, and He is glorified by it because He displays His holiness, which takes action against sin. The Old Testament prophets consistently declared God's impending judgment on the sin of various nations such as Assyria, Babylon, Egypt, Moab, and others. Although God takes no pleasure in the suffering (Ezekiel 18:23, 32; Psalm 5:4; Lamentations 3:33), it is necessary at times because the holy God cannot tolerate sin indefinitely. He will take action against it. Judgment is fittingly identified as God's "alien" or "strange work" by the prophet Isaiah (Isaiah 28:21). As Martin Luther pointed out, if God's justice were ruled as just by human understanding, it would certainly not be divine. It would be merely human justice. Because God is totally incomprehensible and inaccessible to human reason, we must likewise view His justice as such.[46] We can be thankful that God is merciful and doesn't punish to the extent that sin deserves (Psalms 103:10; 130:3).

No matter what calamity occurs, whether it is a result of God's judgment, the fall, the flesh, or the Evil One (or a combination of them), God can turn any bad situation around and bring Himself glory through it. Jesus warned against people's natural tendency to want to label certain occurrences as God's judgment. Remember Jesus said of the Father, "He causes his sun to rise on the evil and the good, and sends rain on the righteous and the unrighteous" (Matthew 5:45). In commenting on the Galileans murdered by Pilate and those who died in the collapse of the Tower of Siloam, Jesus said, "Do you think these Galileans were worse sinners than all the other Galileans because they suffered this way? I tell you, no! But unless you repent, you too will all perish" (Luke 13:1–5). Jesus warned about wrong interpretations, and He did not even provide a divine rationale. What He did was use these tragedies to call people away from their sin and toward God.

PRIDE SQUASHED

God can also allow suffering to humble the proud. One example of this particular type of corrective medicine transformed Nebuchadnezzar, king of Babylon. As the ruler of the most powerful and ruthless nation at that time, Nebuchadnezzar was a king without equal. His military and political influence stretched across most of the civilized world, and his armies crushed many nations. Wise rulers surrendered their riches to the sword of Babylon. The grandeur of his kingdom was reflected in the famous hanging gardens of Babylon, one of the seven wonders of the ancient world.

The story of God's dealing with Nebuchadnezzar is told in Daniel 4:28–37. Nebuchadnezzar became so impressed with his accomplishments that he developed an obscene pride. He acted as if he were a god, but the one true God took action to remind the mighty king that he was only a man. God dealt dementia to Nebuchadnezzar, who for several years lived like a wild animal, feeding on grass and wandering in insanity. By the end of his ordeal, after Nebuchadnezzar had recovered his senses and acknowledged reality, the great king praised the Most High, the living God: "His dominion is an eternal dominion; his kingdom endures from generation to generation" (Daniel 4:34).

As God reveals His great power and person, it squashes the pride and self-sufficiency of mankind. This was the case in Egypt when God imposed plagues upon Egypt. When God hardened the heart of a wicked pharaoh, He merely moved it to continue on according to its bent (Exodus 4:21). God even expressed His reason: "I will gain myself glory through Pharaoh and all his army, and the Egyptians will know that I am the Lord, that there is no other" (see Exodus 7:5,17; 8:10; 14:4). Such humbling can be the avenue that brings hostile hearts toward faith in God.

Suffering can even be a wake-up call. For example, a violent earthquake in Philippi brought one man to salvation. Paul and Silas had been imprisoned in the city jail, and the earthquake broke the bars of the prison. If prisoners escaped, the jailer was held responsible for dereliction of duty, and sentenced to death. In this case, the jailer was about to kill himself. But Paul shouted, "Don't harm yourself!" and he and Silas brought the good news to the man. He and his family believed in Jesus Christ as Lord and Savior (Acts 16:16–34). What could have been a situation of suffering not only for the jailer but for his family turned to joy (verse 34).

Many times God allows suffering to bring a person to a dark place where there is nowhere to look but up. The issue, then, becomes whether or not the person is willing to listen to God.

QUESTIONS
FOR REFLECTION

1. *The author explains the importance of reflecting on "what purposes for the kingdom of God the (difficult) circumstances might be producing." How does the author use the word picture of a kaleidoscope to explain this concept?*

2. *A believer may, with Paul, "boast all the more gladly about my weaknesses so that Christ's power may rest in me" (2 Corinthians 12:9). Why would such a statement sound ridiculous to someone who doesn't know God? Does this concept come naturally for believers?*

3. *See Romans 8:15–17, 2 Corinthians 5:16–17, and 2 Timothy 2:20–21. How do we become useful to God? Must we share in His sufferings in order to share in His joy? Explain.*

4. *Can you recall a time of suffering in your life when you thought, "How can this experience be used to the glory of God?" Conversely, can you recall a time of suffering you wish you had handled differently? Can we waste suffering? Explain.*

"There is a time for everything,
and a season for every activity under heaven:
a time to be born and a time to die,
a time to plant and a time to uproot . . .
A time to weep and a time to laugh,
A time to mourn and a time to dance."

■ Ecclesiastes 3:1–2, 4 ■

WHERE DO WE GO FROM HERE? WALKING THE LIGHTED PATH

MORNING ALWAYS FOLLOWS the darkness of midnight. The first rays of dawn herald the promise of a new day. Though it may have seemed like the night would never end, these first beams remind us that life continues on. The new day is the beginning of an unwritten chapter—a clean slate. Uncharted territory awaits our tread.

Though God may lead us into the valley of deep darkness, He will lead us out. He was guiding our souls even when we were unaware. The darkness cannot hide us from Him, since "even the darkness will not be dark to [Him]" (Psalm 139:12). Gently God moves His children through trials, eventually bringing the awareness that *it is time to move on.*

Long ago, Abraham made a journey of faith when God said to him, "Leave your country, your people and your father's household and go to the land I will show you" (Genesis 12:1). He hadn't asked to be uprooted and go into an unfamiliar territory, but Abraham "obeyed and went, even though he did not know where he was going" (Hebrews 11:8). God had promised him blessing. But what Abraham experienced was severe famines, nasty family feuds and separations, enemy attacks, decades of childlessness (and consequently, an angry wife), and a command to sacrifice his beloved son on a burning altar. There were very dark moments when it was difficult for him to believe, but in the long run, Abraham chose to look to God and trust that He would come through. Periodically, God would remind Abraham of His presence and the generational blessings to come, whispering encouragements like, "Do not be afraid, Abram. I am your shield, your very great reward" (Genesis 15:1).

As a great tangible source of encouragement to you and me, God's Word repeatedly heralds Abraham's faith as an example. *Faith* is the key to keeping in step with God and walking the lighted path. When we believe, the God who led Abraham will also guide us, whether the appointed course is easy or tumultuous. Though God may lead us into the valley of deep darkness, He will lead us out.

The journey onward is deeply rooted in the foundation of faith, which fortifies every step as one moves forward out of the darkness into the healing light. In this chapter, we will identify impediments and potential setbacks that can be anticipated along with ways to combat them as we follow God into uncharted territory.

A LOOK BACK

Before moving on, it may be helpful to remind ourselves of some of the things those who suffer commonly experience in the beginning. At first there is the trauma due to the shock of the actual event or information that caused the suffering. One who encounters suffering will at first be rather numb, anesthetized, to all that is going on around him or her. Shock is said to be the first stage of grief. Shock is a blessing, giving you a change to absorb what is happening. Denial is sometimes part of shock. After a while, anger might surface, as well as such things as inescapable fears, anxiety, extreme loneliness, and powerlessness. It is important at these times to acknowledge the reality of these feelings.

After a time, the search for the meaning of the suffering and what possible benefit might come from it begins. One remembers that suffering in its many forms is part of the reality of life. Many times significant changes in perspective, priorities, and values are forged on the anvil of the experience of pain as one works through the situation. As has been mentioned, pray that this time, as difficult as it is, will not be wasted.

As one moves along, he becomes aware that he is feeling sensitive and vulnerable. Though there are wounds, one must allow the healing of Christ and His love to bring health and strength once again. Change is in progress. The only possible way to move through these days is through the grace of God and the strengthening of the Holy Spirit.

In these early stages of the journey onward, the sufferer has definite needs. It is essential to allow other believers to walk with you at this time. But it is also important to have some time alone. Solitude is of great benefit. Spending time in nature can be very therapeutic as well. To be able to gaze on the panoply of stars on a clear night, the beauty of a flower, or cascades of snow on a mountainside can bring peace. The creation itself points to the Lord.

TURNING THE HEART

Throughout this book, we have seen that the Lord is acquainted with suffering and holds the power to bring victory out of seemingly impossible situations. The most important thing the sufferer can do is turn his heart toward God. The Lord must be the constant focus. The words of the psalmist make it clear that hope is a vital part of the healing process. The Lord alone is the Healer of the broken heart (see Psalm 147:3). The writer of Hebrews encouraged his readers to "fix our eyes on Jesus . . . so that you will not grow weary and lose heart" (Hebrews 12:2–3).

To align ourselves with Him, there is no substitute for communing with God through prayer and spending time in His Word. One of the places where I have spent much time is in the Psalms, finding that they echo the inner cries of my heart.

"Why are you downcast, O my soul? Why so disturbed within me?" (Psalm 42:5). The psalmist's lament is common to anyone who has gone through any sort of suffering, hardship, or trial. He goes on to say, "Put your hope in God, for I will yet praise him." It is important to remember in times of crisis that these times, while difficult and not to be dismissed as unimportant, will pass. The writer of the psalm finds solace by remembering what God has done for him in the past: "My soul is downcast within me; therefore I will remember . . . ," and he recounts times of the Lord's faithfulness to remind him that the Lord will bring him out of this night into the morning as He has so often before. It might even be helpful for us to review God's working in our lives. This practice will help us remember that, though we have been downcast in the past, God brought us through; and as we are again downcast, God will again bring us through.

I can remember lying in the hospital bed having just had a heart attack and the Lord directing my attention to the healing words and vow of Psalm 118:17: "I will not die but live, and proclaim what the LORD has done."

Sometimes truly all you can do is praise the Lord out of obedience. God is found in the praises of His people: "Thou that inhabitest the praises of Israel" (Psalm 22:3 KJV). Though it may be with weak lips, in worship we turn toward Him and declare victory over discouragement. This disarms the Enemy and the lingering vestiges of suffering. God is to be thanked for the good gifts He has given—and even those that have been taken away. He is also to be thanked for the grace that He gives us during suffering, and above all, the gift of Himself and eternity with Him.

Still, the waiting for the pain to pass is one of the biggest challenges for most of us. We are sometimes shocked to see that we haven't grown much beyond the impatience of childhood. And it doesn't help either that we live in a culture that attributes little value to patience. But the Word of God counsels otherwise: "Be still before the LORD and wait patiently for him. . . . Wait for the LORD; be strong and take heart and wait for the LORD" (Psalms 37:7; 27:14). The psalmist lamented that his daily struggle was as intense as the watchman who every night waited for the morning (Psalm 130:1, 5, 6). God does not work on our timetable. Focused waiting anticipates the powerful working of God and in the meantime looks to Him for calm and comfort. Lest we think we are learned "waiters," the theologian Paul Tillich points out the difficulty of *waiting for more of God* often faced by those who become satisfied with their current situations:

> I think of the theologian who does not wait for God, because he possesses Him enclosed within a doctrine. I think of the Biblical student who does not wait for God, because he possesses Him enclosed in a book. I think of the churchman who does not wait for God, because he possesses Him enclosed in an institution. I think of the believer who does not wait for

God, because he possesses Him enclosed within his own experience.[47]

FIGHTING HINDRANCES

Expectant faith that God will answer our cries for help and arm us with the strength we need is vital, especially in the times when the painful reminders of loss and suffering return in full force. People who have had a physical injury or sickness may have recurring aches and pains. A condition like Parkinson's disease slowly progresses and debilitates a once-strong body and mind. War veterans who have experienced combat can experience flashbacks when a loud noise is heard or a certain image takes them back to the battlefield. For those who have lost a loved one, special places and dates on the calendar feel void and empty without the other person's presence. Suffering may not have a defined beginning and end.

Human reactions to pain, such as frustration, anxiety, worry, discontentment, anger, and doubt, are universally experienced and nearly inevitable. A person's flesh and sense of self-entitlement screams at the unfairness of it all. The aftermath of suffering provides a fertile ground for discontentment, which not surprisingly was in the seed of original sin.

We know that with discontentment, sin and suffering came into the world and made it a spiritual battleground. The apostle Paul reminds us that our present struggles are not against flesh and blood but against spiritual forces, and above all our adversary the Devil (Ephesians 6:11–13). As was the case with Job, though his trials were permitted by God, it was Satan who carried them out.

The Devil will remind us of the pain we have been through and tempt us to escape from it through meaningless activity, anger, substances, or anything else that keeps us from turning to God. He hopes to distract us from our purposes as children of God and debilitate our strength. If we become preoccupied with our problems or difficult conditions, we can be hindered from drawing close to God. The suffering, then, is not used to bring glory to God. Because each person impacts the life of others by actions or words, we impact the world around us in a negative way. If a person is spiritually disabled, the influence and testimony of salvation and the resurrection life of redemption through Christ diminishes.

The Enemy is very strong, and if we attempt to fight him on our own, we are in trouble. While we will all have areas of weakness and pain, the power to persevere through the crash points and pressure of character development can come only from the Holy Spirit. With divine enabling, we are able to "bear fruit" and know God's truth (John 15:5). As the apostle John reminds us, "The one who is in you is greater than the one who is in the world" (1 John 4:4), i.e., the Devil.

Fortunately, along with the great gift of God's helping presence, He gives us other people who become embodiments of His love to battle along with us. While time in solitude and rest are necessary, keeping our feelings solely to ourselves can lead to inward focus, depression, and even a martyr complex. Understanding people can share the burden especially by listening and by praying for and together with us. They can also remind us of what is true when despair and the lies of the Enemy creep in. We are not meant to live this life alone but are here to bear one another's burdens (Galatians 6:2).

Rob Bell, a pastor, talks about just being with a person going through a painful time. "Suffering is a place where clichés don't work and words often fail. I was at lunch last week with a friend who is in the middle of some difficult days . . . I can't fix it for him . . . I let him know that I'm in it with him. It isn't very pretty and it isn't very fun, but . . . God is there. . . . Sometimes it means we sit in silence for a while, not knowing what to say. . . . And it is in our suffering together that we find out we are not alone."[48]

While entering into relationships can be extremely difficult after suffering has distanced you from others, there is unique healing that comes from loving your neighbor as yourself. Forging new friendships benefits both you and your neighbor. Openness frees people to share their sufferings and leads to catharsis. Sufferers, then, become wounded healers who share the grace of God.

EMBRACING CONTENTMENT

And what is the evidence that, through Christ, we are overcoming the fallen world? One of the best benchmarks is contentment. When one suffers, questions about the future surface: *Will there ever be joy again? Will things ever be "right" again?* Even while the apostle Paul suffered in prison chains, he wrote a letter of joy to the Philippian believers. "I have learned to be content whatever the circumstances . . . I have learned the secret of being content in any and every situation" (Philippians 4:11–12). Paul's prison cell became a place where the joy of the Lord and praise of God filled the air.

But remember that Paul's contentment was a thing to be "learned." Contentment is a process that does not come instantly. And it's a process that recurs when we're faced with new challenges. It brings growth and maturity into our lives. "Godliness with contentment is great gain" (1 Timothy 6:6).

When Paul speaks of contentment, he is not thinking of resignation and "sucking it in" and bearing with a miserable situation. The Greek word Paul used for *contentment* actually has the idea of sufficiency. This is not the idea of self-sufficiency heralded by our culture or the philosophies of the ancient world. The jewel of Christian contentment is that it is not based on external things. The "secret" of contentment Paul was referring to is listed in Philippians 4:13: "I can do all things through [Christ] who strengthens me" (NASB). It was Christ! Learning contentment means keeping one's desires and focus on Christ. Pain, hardship, loss, solid iron bars, or any other form of confinement do not keep us from Him.

Discontentment festers and spiritual growth is impeded when we focus on the things of this world. But Jesus admonished us to avoid attaching our hearts to earthly things; God knows what we need. Instead, "seek *first* his kingdom" (Matthew 6:33, emphasis added). We learn contentment by asking God for it, practicing it in our daily lives, and above all relying on the power of the Spirit. When this happens, instead of reaching up to grab a higher rung on the ladder of success, there is more reaching down to lift others up and help them closer to the Lord.

STEPS TOWARD WHOLENESS

From this foundation of faith, a person is best able to rebuild his or her life after catastrophe. Not everyone will understand since healing with Christ at the center of all things is different than a simple moving through preconceived stages of grief.

When my wife and I lost our infant son, our hospital-assigned social worker was surprised at how we were handling it. She told us, "You don't fit the model of the stages of grief." Pat and I shared with her how knowing Christ made the difference. Not understanding, she responded, "Well, you are strong people."

We were not strong people. Only because the power and grace of God was at work was it possible not to "grieve like the rest of men, who have no hope" (1 Thessalonians 4:13).

While it is essential to note that healing from tragic circumstances is anything but simple, the following is a summary of the process of moving forward that I have gone through in the most difficult seasons of my life. Just as the foundation of faith that fuels all healing has to be continually revisited, these kinds of steps are revisited and focused on for varying amounts of time depending on the situation.

1. *Identify the loss.* This involves clearly spelling out just what happened and how life changes as a result. It can be beneficial to write this out on paper since many thoughts and feelings are often present.

2. *Release.* Surrender what was lost into the hands of God, the Creator. Everything good is a gift from God. What was lost was to be cultivated and enjoyed for a time and season. While there is a tendency to hang on and to look back, the Lord wants us to focus on Him and anticipate His provision for the future.

3. *Recognition.* Through the losing, the Lord wants to give a greater gift—the gift of Himself. When God truly gives us Himself, it is permanent. Eternal, abundant life is in Him and is not conditioned upon the physical, material, or other persons. As the Creator, He alone can fill the void.

4. *Accept the gift.* God gives the great gift of Himself for a purpose. A new kind of stewardship and view of life is adopted. The new purpose is in and with Him. In time, He will heal and direct us according to His will.

5. *Embrace the change.* We must recognize that suffering

changes us. As I said to my son when we were talking about the things we had experienced, "I'll never be the same again." Intense suffering has great impact on us personally and emotionally. It is important to identify and embrace the changes—not be ashamed of them. Likewise, it is significant to know that the Lord is the great Potter who is shaping us and forming us into the likeness of Christ—the humble, suffering Savior (2 Corinthians 3:18; Galatians 4:19). The dynamic of the Christian is the constant awareness of "who I am in Christ."

Building and rebuilding one's worldview based on identity in Christ is painful, but it is also worth it. God is faithful to help overcome challenges that seem insurmountable. Through pain, we come to depend on God and see His involvement come into view in ways we never would outside of adversity. We begin to see the big picture, and then we can see where God would have us join in what He is doing. Remember that God is always at work in the world and in your life. When He reveals to you what He is doing, He has invited you to join Him.[49] You can be sure your trial will not be wasted.

WHAT IS THE FUTURE TO BRING?

You and I have a choice.

The disciples of Jesus had a choice, too, and for a time following the crucifixion, they surrendered to fear. They were devastated by the painful realization that their Messiah was dead. Paralyzed by emotional shock, they retreated to their homes. They forgot the miracles Jesus performed across Galilee. They forgot the prophecies in the Old Testament. They forgot the promises of their Master. Their faith

withered in the face of adversity, and they completely abandoned their call to spread the good news of the kingdom.

Even after they witnessed the resurrected Christ, the disciples didn't assume their mission right away. In spite of
three years of intense training and firsthand experience with
the Son of God, only the power of the Holy Spirit at Pente-
cost and a righteous boldness could compel them to live as
they had been taught. It was this combination that sparked
the fires of Christianity and changed the known world.

When we endure suffering and emerge from times of
crises, we should seek the power of God and boldly continue
where we know He wants us to go. God's purpose is not for
us to be happy or rich or eternally young. His purpose is to
bring us closer to the image of His Son and to have us share
in the expansion of the kingdom. Everything else is peripheral. If we let suffering take a controlling position on our decision making, we are effectively saying that how we feel is
more important than God's directives. That was the original
mistake of Adam and Eve: listening to their feelings at the
expense of God's command.

As we have seen, when the tendency to focus on the past
surfaces, there are accompanying feelings and emotions that
threaten to slow us down. But if we recognize that God is
greater than all things, then these feelings will not cripple us
permanently. By focusing on God's love and His ultimate
purposes for us—becoming like Him, loving others, and
spreading the good news, being members of the family of
God forever—we find hope, strength, and purpose to carry
on. It is vital for us to draw near to God and discern His specific directions and purpose for our future. As He takes great
pains to transform us, He has a mission that only we can accomplish because He has shaped us precisely for it. Only in
the pursuit of that goal in life is there real joy. Then the

suffering is defeated, it is turned on itself, and it becomes a stepping-stone to giving God greater and greater glory.

While we remain in a world that stands in bewilderment about Christ, we *can choose to bring the truth about who He really is.* When a believer has suffered, there is a witness to the world of the inexplicable power of Christ at work in the person. Our transformation is cause for great joy to the true Christian. A new and different person has emerged, never to be the same again. While we are a work in progress, in the process God promises His followers "a spirit of power, of love and of self-discipline" (2 Timothy 1:7).

QUESTIONS
FOR REFLECTION

1. What is the "uncharted territory" that awaits our tread?

2. See Psalm 42:5–6. What is the psalmist remembering? How can this remembering help us when we're suffering?

3. Review Paul Tillich's quote on waiting for God. How does each of the four characters find difficulty in waiting for God?

4. What steps toward wholeness does the author chronicle? Describe a time in your life when you have taken these steps through a time of crisis.

"For I do not seek to understand
so that I may believe;
but I believe so that
I may understand.
For I believe this also,
that 'unless I believe,
I shall not understand.'"

■ ANSELM OF CANTERBURY ■

IN
CONCLUSION

AS WE HAVE TRAVELED through the unmapped darkness, it has become apparent that suffering is a part of life for us all. The sky can become cloud covered, followed by dark storms that engulf a person in darkness. When we come back into the light, it is important to reflect back on the journey and remember the things learned in the shadows.

PART OF THE PICTURE

Whether caused by the forces of nature in a fallen world, or by the sinful nature of man, or the scheming of the Evil One, pain and trouble are often unexpected companions on our journey. The realities of life make us aware of our creatureliness and our bond with all people—even all creation.

Suffering is like many of God's mysterious and awesome works. As one views the Grand Canyon, it must be viewed from various vantage points. No one view is enough and no one can see it from all its points. Suffering is similar. Only as we realize this can we begin to make sense of the suffering we know. We are skilled at making images of God to our own liking and trying to remove the eternal mystery from the ineffable God. One of the positive effects of suffering is that it can bring down our idols and bring us into a humble pursuit of the living God.

As Diogenes Allen pointed out, "There are many routes which lead to an encounter with the divine realm and to a knowledge of God's presence, and nearly all of these involve facing the harsh and painful realities of life."[51] In the darkness we begin to perceive more clearly the light. In the midst of the man-made lights of the city, it is difficult to see the glory of the moon and stars at night. But in the darkness, the beauty of these reflectors of light is known. He is there! He is at work! He is in control though all seems chaos.

COMMANDING OUR ATTENTION

In the darkness God comes, calls, and draws us into Himself. The Holy Spirit will do what is necessary to help us accept the simple truths of the universe:

> We are weak, He is strong.
> We are mortal, He is immortal.
> We are imperfect, He is perfect.
> We are sinful, He is holy.
> We are finite, He is infinite.
> We suffer, He is sufficient.

Pain and suffering bring these aspects of reality out from the theological chalkboard and directly into our lives. In contrast to the wise person who learns from tragic circumstances, a foolish person refuses to accept his weakness, mortality, and sinfulness and demands a certain "happy" way of life. He believes he is capable of determining his destiny and deludes himself into a myth of self-sufficiency. In doing so, he denies the truth and declares war on God. Rebelling against the unpleasant facts of life and eternity, he may eventually turn his back on his Creator. So instead of seeking the road to God, the one who is not wise will completely abandon the lighted path when faced with difficulty. But a humble disciple recognizes his perceived self-sufficiency is an illusion. He may consider the truths of the universe, and then be driven to the foot of the cross because he realizes he has no solution to his problem of a fallen world.

In the light of His presence we begin to understand that sin is the ultimate cause of all suffering. It is only in the context of suffering that we can understand the mystery of divine love. Though the Scriptures expose the fall as the cause of suffering, the main focus is on God's provision of the cure through His own suffering. God entered the suffering world in the person of Jesus Christ. Through Christ He defeated death itself and robbed it of its power. Now we can begin to make sense of our situations. Through His entering into the hour of darkness (Luke 22:53), He provided an eternal salvation. He is the way, the only way, to the Father's kingdom—to life without darkness (John 14:6). Christ is the "light of the world," and He wants to be our light and walk with us through the darkness (John 8:12). To reject His light and depend on oneself is like trying to find one's way by lighting a match in the howling wind and darkness of a tornado. Hopelessness, despair, death are certain! Whether in darkness or light, you must ask, "In what am I really trusting?"

A NEW KINGDOM

Christ's light leads the disciple on a journey, a pathway, to what John Bunyan called "the celestial city" in *The Pilgrim's Progress*. With the psalmist, the person of faith can boldly say, "The Lord is my light and my salvation; whom shall I fear? The Lord is the strength of my life; of whom shall I be afraid?" (Psalm 27:1 KJV). Through faith and the power of God, one can know the great loving heart of our Lord.

God not only gives strength for the journey and the light of His presence, but He also unites us to Himself. When we hit the head of a nail with a hammer, the force of that blow is transmitted into the point. Serious affliction, which involves physical pain, distress of soul, and social degradation all at once, is like a nail whose point pierces the center of the heart. That kind of nail pierced the heart of God on the cross. And the infinite distance between God and man is crossed by it. Simone Weil concluded, "Affliction is a marvel of divine technique. He whose soul remains ever turned toward God, though the nail pierces it, finds himself nailed to the very center of the universe. It is the true center; it is not the middle; it is beyond space and time; it is God."[52]

It is, then, vital to constantly fix one's focus on the Lord and resist all the distractions in this world. Solomon said that the wise are found in the house of mourning and the fool is found in the house of petty laughter (Ecclesiastes 7:2–6).

What good can come from being in the house of mourning? Bill Hendricks lost his wife, Nancy, to cancer. He states, "Somehow, during my stay at the House of Mourning, all the truths I've ever known about God have become more true than I'd ever imagined, and true in ways that I haven't even seen. Make no mistake. Nancy's death has hurt more than I have described. Nor does the hurt just go away. But I'll say this: God has shown up for me, as He did for her, and for my daughters. . . . His lovingkindness is everlasting. I have found that to be a true statement. I can trust that."[53]

The wise know and accept their limitations and their destiny, while the fool prefers to ignore and ridicule the obvious. This does not mean that Christians should never be joyful or have happiness in their souls. Instead, we can find our joy in the vast richness of God and rejoice with the things that please Him.

In the seemingly hopeless hour of grief over the loss of her brother, Lazarus, Jesus told Martha, "If you believe, you will see the glory of God" (John 11:40 NASB). All along Jesus had planned to raise Lazarus from the dead. Despite deep grief, how many souls were affected by this display of Christ's power? The power of God is available in our lives here and now, and that power will also raise us to be with Him in the age to come (1 Corinthians 6:14; Ephesians 1:18–21).

FINAL HOPE

A right disposition of the heart will be accompanied by a continual seeking and searching to know God. If you cease, you will set yourself up for great peril. Though the Master Craftsman brings us into the fire, He knows what He is doing. He will bring us out as a masterpiece fit for His use and glory. This is the way of the working of the Lord as expressed in Psalm 66:8–12: "For you, O God, tested us; you refined us like silver" (verse 10). Few will experience the immensity of Job's suffering, but he knew his destiny to come: "I will come forth as gold" (Job 23:10). The courageous nature of faith is revealed through steps made in the dark. First steps may be a bit tentative, but they must be taken. Each step will grow stronger.

Everyone knows another day will come. At any given point in our lives, we will have either just come through suffering, be presently suffering, or be on the brink of entering suffering. This is not the end of the journey, undoubtedly there will be more tests for our faith to come. The main issue we all face is: Are we ready? How will we respond? Though we'll never be perfectly prepared, we can review what we and others have learned in prior darkness. What will you take with you that will sustain you in the future? Though God may not give a lot of answers, He will give us more of Himself, which is the greatest need we have.

In knowing the Lord and His victory over suffering through suffering, we have hope and power to persevere, with joy, on the journey. In the darkness, as a silhouette, the image of God begins to take shape. One day the dark clouds over all creation will finally break up. What was unmapped darkness will be filled with the glorious light of Christ's presence (Isaiah 60:1–2).

In and with Christ will we arrive secure and safe at last in the celestial city of heaven. Once someone is in the kingdom, he or she is in for all of eternity. Nothing can take away God's love and eternal blessing, and we will be worshiping and rejoicing with the angels and fellow children of God in His family forever. Then the words of the prophecy will be the ultimate reality: "He will wipe every tear from their eyes. There will be no more death or mourning or crying or pain, for the old order of things has passed away" (Revelation 21:4).

Amidst the darkness, God has called His people to be bearers of the good news of the light of Christ to fellow pilgrims (Matthew 5:14–16; Philippians 2:15). This is our highest calling in spite of the increased suffering it may bring. Knowing God, making His glory known, and doing His work occupies us. This is all the beginning, the preparation, for the great day when with the choirs of heaven we proclaim:

> *Hallelujah! For the Lord God omnipotent reigns!*
> *And He shall reign forever and ever!*

In the darkness, the light of His presence has beamed into our hearts. As you pass through the seasons of life with their struggles and sorrows, the question comes, *What will you focus on?*

What do you know because you've walked with God through the darkness? Will you continue to search and seek to know this awesome and mysterious God? One day you will see and know Him in unrestrained fullness.

Will you trust and follow Him in the darkness? In the light?

Will you love other sojourners, all people, and relate as a fellow sufferer? Will you help them find abundant life in Christ? And love enough to suffer with them as Christ entered our darkness to bring us light?

If so, the beams of hope, joy, and strength will shine through you as you are led on your journey toward the Light.

QUESTIONS
FOR REFLECTION

1. How is "suffering like many of God's mysterious and awesome works"?

2. Contrast the way a wise and a foolish man respond to suffering.

3. Why is the "continual seeking and searching to know God" so vital?

4. The author concludes that "what was unmapped darkness will be filled with the glorious light of Christ's presence." Explain his metaphor of the image of God as a silhouette in the darkness.

NOTES

Chapter 1: The Storm: What in the World Is Going On?

1. Charles Scobie, *The Ways of Our God* (Grand Rapids: Eerdmans, 2003), 659.

2. Evelyn M. Sompson, ed., *John Donne's Sermons on the Psalms and Gospels* (Berkeley: University of California Press, 2003), 243.

3. Francis Schaeffer, *The God Who Is There* (Downers Grove, Ill.: InterVarsity, 1968), 128–30.

Chapter 2: Disturbances: Reality As We Know It

4. Gerhard Sauter, *Gateway to Dogmatics* (Grand Rapids: Eerdmans, 2003), 238–39.

5. Edith Schaeffer, *L'Abri* (Wheaton: Crossway, 1992), 98.

6. Simone Weil, *Waiting for God* (New York: Perennial Classics, 2001), 71.

7. M. Scott Peck, *People of the Lie* (New York: Simon & Schuster, 1983), 69–84.

8. Kevin J. Vanhoozer, *First Theology* (Downers Grove, Ill.: InterVarsity, 2002), 22. (These are Vanhoozer's comments on Cupitt.)

9. H. Seebass, *(nepes)*, in *Theological Dictionary of the Old Testament*, G. J. Botterweck, H. Ringgren, H. J. Fabry eds., vol IX (Grand Rapids: Eerdmans, 1998), 508.

10. C. S. Lewis, *A Grief Observed* (San Francisco: Harper, 1961), 66.

11. Dorothee Soelle, *Suffering*, trans. Everett R. Kalin (Philadelphia: Fortress, 1975), 66.

12. Lewis, *A Grief Observed*, 66.

13. Hans Kung, *Gott und Das Leid*, Theologische Meditationen 18 (Zurich: Venziger Verlag, 1967), 37.

14. Philip Yancey, *Rumors* (Grand Rapids: Zondervan, 2003), 50.

15. Blaise Pascal, *Pensees*, trans. J. Krailsheimer (London: Penguin Books, 1995), 122, 45.

16. Peck, *People of the Lie*, 69–84.

17. Pascal, *Pensees*, 122, 45.

18. Lewis, *A Grief Observed*, 66.

Chapter 3: Who Is the Sovereign God? A Very Present Power

19. Paul Enns, *The Moody Handbook of Theology* (Chicago: Moody, 1989), 186.

20. Weil, *Waiting on God*, 139.

21. Karl Barth, *Church Dogmatics*, vol. II, part I, trans. T. H. L. Parker et al., ed. G. W. Bromiley and T. F. Torrance (Edinburgh: T&T Clark, 1957), 349.

22. J. R. R. Tolkien, *The Return of the King*, 2nd ed. (Boston: Houghton Mifflin, 1965), 246.

23. David Wells, *God in the Wasteland* (Grand Rapids: Eerdmans, 1994), 136, 144–45.

24. Rudolf Otto, *The Idea of the Holy*, trans. John W. Harvey (London: Oxford University Press, 1958).

25. A. W. Tozer, *Knowledge of the Holy* (San Francisco: Harper & Row, 1961), 82.

26. Charles Hodge, *Systematic Theology*, vol. 1 (Grand Rapids: Eerdmans, 1968), 247.

27. http://en.wikipedia.org/wiki/Metanarrative (accessed 13 October 2005).

28. Meir Sternberg, *The Poetics of Biblical Narrative* (Bloomington: Indiana University Press, 1985), 101.

29. Paul Helm, *The Providence of God* (Downers Grove, Ill.: InterVarsity, 1994), 196.

30. Barth, *Church Dogmatics*, 572.

31. Edith Schaeffer, *The Tapestry* (Waco: Word, 1981), 14–15.

Chapter 4: Out of the Darkness: How Jesus Makes a Difference

32. S.v. "Providence," in *Dictionary of Biblical Imagery*, Leland Ryken, James C. Wilhoit, Tremper Longman III, eds. (Downers Grove, Ill.: InterVarsity, 1998), 682.

33. Henri Blocher, *Evil and the Cross*, trans. David Preston (Downers Grove, Ill.: InterVarsity, 1994), 133.

34. Pascal, *Pensees*, 289.

35. Marcus M. Wells, "Holy Spirit, Faithful Guide"

Chapter 5: Riding It Out: The Value of Suffering

36. Richard Swinburne, *Providence and the Problem of Evil* (Oxford: Clarendon, 1998), 244–45.

37. http://www.americanrhetoric.com/speeches/bgrahammemorialgo.htm (accessed 1 November 2005).

38. C. S. Lewis, *The Problem of Pain* (New York: Macmillan, 1962), 93.

39. Corrie ten Boom, *The Hiding Place* (Old Tappan, N.J.: Revell, 1971), 150, 195.

40. Augustine, *The City of God*, trans. Henry Bettenson (London: Penguin Books, 1984), book IV, chapter 13, 573.

41. Peter Kreeft, *Making Sense Out of Suffering* (Ann Arbor, Mich.: Servant Books), 78.

42. C. S. Lewis, *Weight of Glory* rev. ed. (New York: Touchstone, 1996), 26.

43. W. Schrage, and E. S. Berstenberger, *Suffering*, trans. John E. Steely (Nashville: Abingdon, 1980), 209.

44. Joni Tada and Steve Estes, *When God Weeps* (Grand Rapids: Zondervan, 1997), 137.

45. Julian of Norwich, *Revelations of Divine Love* (London: Penguin Books, 1998), 71–72.

46. Otto, *Idea of the Holy*, 101.

Chapter 6: Where Do We Go from Here? Walking the Lighted Path

47. Paul Tillich, *The Shaking of the Foundations* (New York: Scribner, 1948), 150.

48. Rob Bell, *Velvet Elvis* (Grand Rapids: Zondervan, 2005), 170.

49. Henry T. Blackaby and Claude V. King, *Experiencing God* (Nashville: Broadman & Holman, 2004), 52, 55.

In Conclusion

50. Anselm of Canterbury, *The Major Works*, *Proslogion*, Brian Davis and G. R. Evans, eds. (Oxford: University Press, 1998), 87.

51. Diogenes Allen, *The Traces of God in a Frequently Hostile World* (Cowley Publications, 1981), 13.

52. Weil, *Waiting for God*, 81.

53. William Hendricks, *The Light That Never Dies* (Chicago: Northfield, 2005), 131–32, 136.

THE LIGHT THAT NEVER DIES

A Story of Hope in the Shadows of Grief

ISBN: 1-881273-69-5

In the prime of his life, William Hendricks surrendered his wife to breast cancer. Yet he could say, "Give thanks to the Lord, for He is good." In a warm gentle style, Bill Hendricks shares God's goodness, not just even in the midst of suffering, but especially in that personal pain.

"I cannot remember the last time I was moved as deeply by a book . . . I will never look at human suffering the same way."
—Peggy Wehmeyer, host, "The World Vision Report,"
Former religion correspondent, ABC News

www.MoodyPublishers.com